How to Talk to Anyone

Defeat Social Anxiety, Make Better Small Talk, and Communicate Effectively

Joseph Miretti

© **Copyright 2023 - All rights reserved.**

The content contained within this book may not be reproduced, duplicated or transmitted without direct written permission from the author or the publisher.

Under no circumstances will any blame or legal responsibility be held against the publisher, or author, for any damages, reparation, or monetary loss due to the information contained within this book,eit her directly or indirectly.

Legal Notice:

This book is copyright protected. It is only for personal use. You cannot amend, distribute, sell, use, quote or paraphrase any part, or the content within this book, without the consent oft he author or publisher.

DisclaimerNot ice:

Please note the information contained within this document is for educational and entertainment purposes only. All effort has been executed to present accurate, up to date, reliable, complete information. No warranties of any kind are declared or implied. Readers acknowledge that the author is not engaged in the rendering of legal, financial, medical or professional advice. The content within this book has been derived from various sources. Please consult a licensed professional before attempting any techniques outlined in this book.

By reading this document, the reader agrees that under no circumstances is the author responsible for any losses, direct or indirect, that are incurred as a result of the use of the information contained within this document, including, but not limited to, errors, omissions, or inaccuracies.

Table of Contents

INTRODUCTION 1

CHAPTER 1: A CRITICAL SKILL 7
   WHY COMMUNICATION MATTERS 9
      Relationship Building 10
      It Opens Doors 11
      Builds Your Character 12
      Creative Self-Expression 12
      Become an Effective Leader 13
   COMMUNICATION AT WORK 13
      Employees Are More Productive 14
      Effectively Improves Crisis Situations 15
      Communication Equals Knowledge 16
      Learning to Work Together 16
      Employees Feel Like They Have a Voice 17
   EFFECTS OF POOR COMMUNICATION SKILLS 18
      Poor Communication: What to Look For 18
   REASONS FOR YOUR STRUGGLES 20
   WHY SOCIAL ANXIETY? 21
   WHY SHOULD YOU TALK TO ANYONE? 22
   SELF-REFLECTION QUESTIONS 24

CHAPTER 2: STEP ONE—LETTING YOURSELF SHINE 27
   YOUR SELF-ESTEEM HAS A SAY 29
      Your Core Beliefs 29
      Where Does Low Self-Esteem Come From? 30
      The Voice Within 31
      History Repeats Itself 32
      Connection Between Self-Esteem and Poor Communication 33
   DRESS TO IMPRESS 33
      Dressing More Confidently 34
   FROM BODY IMAGE TO BODY LANGUAGE 38
      Body Image and Social Communication 39
      Improving Your Body Image 40

BEING YOURSELF WITH SOCIAL ANXIETY 42
    Shift the Way You Think *43*
    Offer Yourself Compassion *44*
    Create an Action Plan *45*
    Put Yourself in Uncomfortable Situations *46*
CONFIDENCE BUILDING TIPS 47
    Accomplish What You Need to Do *47*
    Acknowledge Your Progress *47*
    Have No Fear *48*
    Advocate for Yourself *49*
    Who Cares What They Think? *49*
SELF-AFFIRMATIONS 50
    Self-Affirmations for Boosting Confidence *53*
STEP ONE ACTION STEPS 54

CHAPTER 3: STEP TWO—STARTING FROM WITHIN **57**

NEGATIVE THOUGHTS AND COMMUNICATION 58
    How Are Your Negative Thoughts Holding You Back? *59*
    Changing Your Negative Thoughts *60*
    How to Stop Your Negative Thoughts *62*
    Overcoming Negative Thought Patterns *65*
THE INNER VOICE 68
    Befriending Your Inner Critic *69*
SELF-CARE FOR SELF-CONFIDENCE 72
    Talking to Yourself Positively *73*
    Eating Healthy *74*
    Getting Enough Sleep *75*
    Maintain a Workout Schedule *76*
    Have Fun *77*
    Laugh *79*
    Creativity Is Key *80*
SMILING AS A POSITIVE ATTITUDE 81
    Benefits to Smiling *82*
SELF-AFFIRMATIONS FOR POSITIVE THINKING 83
STEP TWO ACTION STEPS 84

CHAPTER 4: STEP THREE—MAKING AN IMPRESSION **87**

STRIKING A CONVERSATION 89
    Is It True? *90*
    Is It Helpful? *91*
    Is It Inspiring? *92*

Is It Necessary? *93*
Is It Kind? *94*
STARTING A CONVERSATION 95
Introduce Yourself *96*
Offer Them Compliments *96*
Talk About the Weather *97*
Ask Open-Ended Questions *98*
Ask For Help *98*
SETTING THE TONE IN CONVERSATIONS 99
Condescending Tone *100*
Boredom Tone *101*
Supportive and Empathetic Tone *102*
READING BODY LANGUAGE 103
Do We Really Pay Attention to Body Language? *104*
Become Magnetic to Others *104*
The Importance of Eye Contact *106*
MAKING A GREAT FIRST IMPRESSION AND MEANINGFUL CONNECTION 107
SELF-AFFIRMATIONS TO EASE CONVERSATION ANXIETY 110
STEP THREE ACTION STEPS 111

CHAPTER 5: STEP FOUR—KEEP IT GOING 113

ASKING THE RIGHT QUESTIONS 114
Asking "Why" *115*
What Happens if You're New? *116*
Think Outside the Box *116*
TIPS TO HAVE A MEMORABLE CONVERSATION 117
Ask Thought-Provoking Questions *117*
Pay Attention *118*
Share Personal Stories *118*
TYPES OF QUESTIONS TO ASK 119
Open-Ended Versus Closed-Ended Questions *119*
Superlative Questions *120*
Challenging Questions *120*
ACTIVE LISTENING 121
Active Listening Is? *122*
Why Is Active Listening Important? *124*
Improving Your Active Listening Skills *125*
KEEP THE CONVERSATION FLOWING 127
What Is Conversation Flow? *127*
Tips to Keep a Conversation Going *128*
SELF-AFFIRMATIONS FOR CONVERSATION FLOW 129

- Step Four Action Steps 130

CHAPTER 6: STEP FIVE—A MASTER COMMUNICATOR 133
- The Power of Language 135
  - Language and Culture 135
  - Language and Business 136
  - Language and Personal Development 137
  - Language and Personal Interaction 137
- Types of Language 138
  - Oral/Written 138
  - Denotative/Connotative 138
- Language Elements 139
  - Clarity 140
  - Word Economy 140
  - Obscene Remarks 141
  - Odd/Unfamiliar Language 141
  - Influential Language 142
  - Mixing It Up 142
- Disagreeing Without Disrespecting 142
  - Be Open to Another Perspective 143
  - Show Humility 143
  - Keep an Open Mind 143
  - Don't Go Into Attack Mode 144
  - Breathe Before Speaking 144
- Dealing With Challenging People 145
  - Stop Trying to Change Them 146
  - Understand Where They're Coming From 146
  - Offer Them Respect 146
  - Use It as a Lesson 147
- Self-Affirmations for Master Communication 147
- Step Five Action Steps 148

CONCLUSION 149

REFERENCES 153

Introduction

Lifebe ginsatth e end of your comfort zone. –Ne aleDonaldWals h

I remember when I met my partner's friends for the first time. The awkward moments I experienced—it felt like I was a fish out of the water, struggling to gasp for air. Conversations with people felt like the most uncomfortable experience. My nerves skyrocketed out of control, and I couldn't help but wonder the same question that anyone in my situation would ask: *What do they think of me?*

That question always turned my world upside down. When I didn't know how to answer it, I felt my confidence drain deep downint ot he pit of my stomach.

Hi, my name is Joseph and I have social anxiety. Man, it feels good to say that out loud to people who can relate to what I'm goingt hrough.

I've felt socially anxious for many years of my life. Awkward is the way I would describe it. Socially awkward. I have three sons, and at times, I still feel awkward speaking to other parents at their birthday parties. But I'm getting better; I'm learning to step outside my comfort zone to gain the confidence I need in publicse ttings.

This book was written specifically for you, who also feels socially awkward, and who allows worry about the future to keep you awake when you're trying to go to sleep. Your mind doesn'tquit .

What if they don't like me?

Iwonde rwh atth ey think of me.

What if my poor communication skills prevent me from getting a better job?

What if I always feel misunderstood due to my lack of confidence in social settings?

All these *what-if* questions boggle your mind every day. You feel like you need to prove yourself to everyone, and if you don't, you won't be able to grow your circle of friends and you'll be left pining for yourself, alone, shy, and misunderstood.

Don't worry—I've felt that way too. It's not fun being in our shoes, which is exactly why I wrote this book. You no longer have to feel this way; you have the potential to step outside your comfort zone and gain the confidence and self-esteem you need to rock your conversations.

As you go through this book, I encourage you to ask yourself these questions. It is important that you're truly honest with yourself—honesty leads to clarity, and clarity leads to permanent transformation.

"DoIst ruggle with poor self-confidence?"

"Do I feel inferior and don't feel like I can do what others can?"

"AmIove rlyshy ?"

"DoIhave trouble keeping up with the flow of conversation?"

"AmIne rvoust ot alkt ope ople?"

"DoIc onstantly feel misunderstood?"

"DoIst ruggle with sharing my message clearly?"

If you answered yes to many of these questions, you are experiencing social anxiety, and that's okay. We are going through this journey together—you don't need to feel alone anylonge r.

This book is like the book of confidence, so to speak. It is going to help transform your life. I know this because the strategies I share in this book have also changed my life. I know it can offer permanent transformation and healing to anyone who reads it and understands itsw isdom.

Asy oudive int ore ading,y ou'lle arnsomany things, such as:

- understanding the most critical skill you need to effectively help you in social settings

- how to increase your self-confidence and the way you view yourself every day

- how to rewire negative thinking patterns, shift your mindset, and challenge your inner critic

- the importance of making a good impression and how to do it so people remember your confidence

- what to do in order to keep the conversation smooth andflow ing

- how to become a master communicator

Learning these skills will not only up-level your confidence, but they will help you step out of your shell so you can become a master at communicating your message. Prior to this book, you may have lost hope. You may have felt that your struggle with social anxiety was hopeless and that you will never catch your break. I want you to know something—even though you are shy and experience negative thoughts that distract you from living your dream life, it doesn't have to be the end. Let me rephrase that—it doesn't have to be the end of your book, but it can be the end of a chapter in your journey.

I remember all those moments when I also felt socially anxious. Frustration overtook me and I felt angry at myself that I couldn't get past the awkward stage. I learned something about this journey—I can choose to stay there and let social anxiety control my life, or I can choose to move forward and acquire the skills I need to become a phenomenal communicator.

Now, I am offering this choice to you. What do you choose? I can only hazard a guess that since you are reading this book, you've chosen to become the second person—the one who is willing to understand the art of communicating so you can go after the life of your dreams.

Nowasky ourselft his:Why didy ouc hoose to buy this book?

Chances are, you've reached your limit of being socially awkward. You want better, and you know you deserve better. You know you cannot progress in your life, career, or relationship unless you overcome social anxiety. You cannot help but think of so many wasted opportunities you've let pass by because you struggled with being sociable, so you're done living this way. You want to live a happy, fulfilling life, but you knowit 'snot possible unle ssy oufe el positive and empowered.

These are pretty good reasons to want to make a change in your life and personal development. Remember your *why* as you dive into the remaining chapters. These reasons will keep you going and help you move forward so you are not only reaching the light at the end of a socially awkward tunnel but receiving all that is meant for you because you have become confident enough to go after it.

I am grateful that you are on this journey with me. I trust that the content in this book helps you transform your life in a way that you cannot possibly imagine. There will be a day when you are in the middle of a business meeting or even at your kid's birthday party, and you become the life of the party. You have so much confidence within you that people gravitate toward your energy.

I am looking forward to that day for you. Until then, keep going. Keep choosing to understand yourself and keep growing and evolving. Here's to the next step of your journey. You got this.

Chapter 1:

A Critical Skill

Poor communication is not only increasing stress and decreasing morale, but it is also directly impacting companies' bottom line. –Abbey Lunney

A recent study by the State of Business Communication demonstrates a significant loss of dollars every year due to poor communication. I am not talking about thousands of dollars—I'm talking about *trillions*! In fact, $1.2 trillion, to be exact. This means that over twelve thousand dollars per employee are lost every single year (Grammarly, 2022)!

Some people may not think communication is important, but this study shows that it is. Many other instances clearly demonstrate that communication is imperative in every area of our lives:

- Ineffective company communication causes workplace anxiety for 80% of US employees (*11 remarkable workplace communications statistics to know*, 2022).

- Poor communication is responsible for 70% of corporate errors (Beene Garter, 2022).

- 67.5 percent of all marriages fail due to poor communication (American Academy of Matrimonial Lawyers, 2019).

- Effective team communication may see at least a 25% increase in productivity (*Communication Statistics in the Workplace 2022*, 2022).

When there is poor communication, especially in the workplace, we inhibit negative feelings toward ourselves and our coworkers. We may feel anxious as if we're not doing our job correctly. We may feel that our teammates don't like us because they rarely speak to us. And we may feel unproductive because our boss is not explaining the project efficiently.

Poor communication can cost us not only dollars in the workplace but it can cost us our mental health.

What happens when we don't get along with our team members due to a lack of communication? We feel alone, judged, and misunderstood. We feel anxious and, at times, depressed. We feel like we want to hide in a corner and not go to work, and we start to dislike our job. When all of this happens, the company's bottom line suffers because we don't feel like doing our job, we're not productive, or we simply don't feel like a valuable asset. When our mental health is low, the company suffers a great loss not just in dollars but in employee retention. It is important for employers to keep their employees happy and fulfilled so they can continue doing an excellent job. Whene mployees are happy, business continues booming.

Thisc hapter will prepare you for a few things:

- how to build trust and relationships by understanding the art of communication

- how effective communication can open up an array of opportunities

- how communication can help solve conflicts effectively

- how the way you communicate can develop your personality and build your character

- how effective employer communication can enhance employee satisfaction and fulfillment

- how the art of communication can help you talk with anyone you desire, regardless of their stature

At the end of the chapter, I'll offer you a few questions that you can reflect on so you can start taking action on your communication skills right away. I encourage you to answer these questions truthfully in a notebook or a journal if you have one. These questions will help you increase your self-confidence and instill a positive mindset so you can begin communicating with ease.

Why Communication Matters

Everywhere you go, people are communicating. Your friends and loved ones are talking amongst themselves about what they did the night before. Your boss is emailing your team to let them know the daily tasks. Your coworkers are discussing the annual revenue projections and what is needed to reach the monthly goal. Your family is discussing what to have for dinner tonight.

We communicate all the time. According to Merriam-Webster, the scientific definition of communication is the "art of transferring information; an exchange of information per se" (2023).

There are three different ways to communicate our message:

- **Written:** Written communication is in the form of an email or letter. Any information you physically write to another person is considered to be written communication. When you journal, you relay information to yourself, which is also written communication.

- **Verbal:** When you are physically speaking with someone, either face to face or through the telephone. You're engaging in conversation with another person in ordert oge t your message across.

- **Non-verbal:** This is where the phrase *actions speak louder than words* comes in handy. Many people use non-verbal communication to express how they're feeling. Their legs could be crossed toward the other person. They could be flirting with their eyes or be engrossed in the conversation by sitting up straight.

The way you communicate makes a huge difference in its effectiveness. If you use non-verbal communication without intending to, you might send the wrong message to the other person. There are certain ways that people receive the message you're putting out—it is important you are aware of how you are expressing yourself.

In learning to communicate more effectively, it is important to firstle arnhow to do so, and here's why:

Relationship Building

Mastering your communication skills is one of the main components when building and fostering powerful relationships in your life and business. If you are in a relationship with your partner and you never communicate, how will the relationship work? How will it strive and press forwardw ith love, trust, and support?

Making communication part of your relationship can ensure longevity, empathy, and mutual trust. We can't do things alone—well, we can, but it will take a lot longer to accomplish—so having people to communicate with can make working on a project less stressful and overwhelming.

Mastering effective communication skills can also help in times of conflict. For instance, if you're arguing with your partner about financial issues, knowing how to communicate effectively so that your partner understands your reasoning can help resolve the issue efficiently. You may want to get your point across and will say whatever you can to ensure that happens, but it is also severely important to listen to the other party's point of view. If not, they may feel unseen and unheard, which can cause unnecessary animosity. It is more than okay to be quiet when the situation calls for it so that you can listen effectively and wait for your turn.

It Opens Doors

Learning how to communicate can open more doors for you than you could possibly imagine. For example, if you know how to speak to others about your product or service, your business can skyrocket with amazing clients and other extraordinary, once-in-a-lifetime opportunities. If you know how to sell yourself in an interview, you could land the job of your dreams.

Doors that may feel impossible to open can open if you learn how to share your message effectively. Strong communicators know how to present themselves well and effectively communicate what they have to offer. Tony Robbins says, "To effectively communicate, we must realize that we are all different in the way we perceive the world and use this understanding as a guide to our communication with others" (n.d.). He also says, "What we do in life is determined by how we communicate to ourselves. In the modern world, the quality oflife ist he quality of communication" (n.d.).

Builds Your Character

As we grow up, we develop a strong sense of self. Our personality develops and we understand our uniqueness compared to others. Being an effective communicator helps you increase your confidence and self-esteem. It helps you develop your personality to greater heights, where you identify who you are and whom you desire to become.

You may find yourself in a situation that you don't like or that makes you uncomfortable. Communication can come in handy, and you can express yourself in a way that communicates your discomfort to the other party. This can help you build a stronger personality and character and become an inspiring role modelt ot hose who are witnessing your growth.

Creative Self-Expression

Learning how to communicate can help you express your individuality and uniqueness. Everyone has an authentic message to share with the world—by learning how to communicate your message, you can reach many people who need to hear it.

When you're at work, you can communicate your vision to your coworkers in a way that makes them excited to help you see it through. People generate creative ideas by brainstorming with their peers and effectively communicating their vision. There is always a lot of back and forth in conversation, which helps the workflow feel smooth.

Become an Effective Leader

To be a powerful leader, you need to learn how to use all forms of communication effectively. Effective leaders know how to ask great questions in order to help with transformation and change. They know how to listen and offer advice when needed to those looking for guidance. They know how to share their message through a social media post, email, or letter that makes their followers think and embrace change.

Your communication skills can set you apart from the rest, making you an influential leader who changes people's lives. It can help you make powerful decisions that are for the betterment of your community. These decisions may not always lead to a resolution you like, but by mastering your communication skills, you can make decisions that result in more positive outcomes. There are many worldwide leaders who know how to communicate their message. They not only speak, but they listen to their people. They are not quick to judge; instead, they use effective non-verbal communication that helps people feel seen and heard.

Communication at Work

If we don't effectively communicate with our coworkers about projects and getting other tasks done, the business can go downhill. It can suffer a huge detriment due to loss of income and clients and due to high employee turnover. What happens if a business is continually struggling in various areas? Potential bankruptcy can occur, which can shut down the business for good.

Communication sounds like a simple area to rectify, but if it isn't, business and everything attached to it can result in a negative domino effect. It is important that we pay attention to how we communicate at work so it can be intentional and solidify relationships with our coworkers so we work together to reach our goals.

So why focus on solidifying workplace communication? Here's why:

Employees Are More Productive

We love motivation and acknowledgment; it's what makes us excited to come to work and be present every day.

According to TeamStage and based on 2022 numbers, here are a few statistics regarding employee motivation:

- When employees are motivated, they are 20% more productive.

- Employee tardiness is reduced by 41% if employees feel motivated to come to work.

- 87% of employees who experience continual motivation by coworkers or superiors are less likely to quit their job.

- Employees who don't feel motivated and engaged can cause up to $550 billion dollars per year in lost business income!

- If employees are motivated to perform their job well, the company can experience 27% higher profit.

If we take these statistics into consideration, we understand that motivation, recognition, and appreciation are vitally important in order to keep us happy so we can perform our job well.

How can we keep ourselves motivated? By hearing our boss' praises that we are doing an amazing job and effectively communicating with our coworkers about project details so we can work as a team to get things done.

Effectively Improves Crisis Situations

When experiencing a physical crisis, it is important we learn how to communicate with all those involved so nothing is lost in translation. Ineffective communication can put a strain on our professional relationship, cause animosity, and throw unnecessary wood into the fire.

Some ways to help you increase communication when experiencing a crisis or when you're helping someone through a crisis situation are:

- **Listen rather than speak.** Listening is a powerful form of communication, so it is important we learn how to effectively listen to the other party rather than blurtout what we want to say.

- **Make it clear that you understand what the other person is going through.** Listen intently and offer advice when needed. Sometimes, someone going through a crisis simply needs to vent to someone who showst hey care. Be that person.

- **Address concerns with logic and rationale.** If you are helping someone going through a crisis, help them see things from a clear perspective. Most often, those experiencing a crisis situation are allowing their emotions to navigate their decisions—act as a mediator and help them decipher the best decision by coming from a logical perspective.

- **Prepare for any possible outcome.** Mentally prepare yourself for the best- and worst-case scenario. Learn how to effectively communicate with your stakeholders and anyone else involved regarding the next steps so you can come to a mutual agreement.

Communication Equals Knowledge

Another word for communication is *sharing*. Sharing knowledge and wisdom with those who desire to learn from you. If we don't share this knowledge, we are doing a disservice to others because it was given to us, so we can give it away.

When we acquire knowledge and successfully teach others what we've learned, they can use that knowledge in a way they deem fit. It not only makes for a better society where we collaborate together, but as societal innovation increases, it constitutes growth and helps many evolve into intelligent human beings.

Learning to Work Together

One of the main goals of team-building workshops is to strengthen communication, collaboration, and partnership. Some of these exercises are proven to be quite challenging; therefore, we need to communicate and ensure we are gearing toward the common goal.

Senior management also uses these workshops to decipher their employee's strengths and weaknesses so they can use their work ethic to the best of their ability. For example, if an employee's weakness is numbers, they would refrain from giving them an accounting task. If they notice that there is an employee who has superb leadership skills, they will give the employee more projects that include overseeing the project fromst art to finish.

Learning to work together effectively is a huge benefit for the company in the long run. The employees are happy because they feel like part of the team, and they're building relationships with their coworkers. This makes it easier to communicate with each other so the business has steady success.

Employees Feel Like They Have a Voice

One of the most important aspects of workplace culture is feeling like we have the opportunity to speak our minds without feeling judged. We are able to use our voices to share our ideas, express our frustrations, and communicate with our coworkers about how we're feeling. This is not always easy, especially when those that we need to speak to are hard-headed and prideful, or our boss is not as open to hearing what we have to say.

If we feel uncomfortable speaking our minds, we dislike going to work, and we feel underappreciated. We shut down and do the bare minimum because we feel, "What's the point?"

Keeping the employees satisfied is just as important as doing whatever we can to keep our clients happy. When our employees are happy and love coming to work, their excitement is reflected in their service, which keeps customers coming back for a long time.

Feeling comfortable communicating with our bosses as well as our coworkers on a regular basis will help our work life feel more pleasurable and satisfactory. Not only can we ensure our voice is being heard and taken into consideration, but we can alsoe nsure that the company knows how valuable we truly are.

Effects of Poor Communication Skills

Poor communication skills can not only make us anxious, but they can also affect our relationships with others.

If you're trying to resolve a conflict and the other party simply does not want to be receptive, the conversation can feel uncomfortable. It can feel like a waste of time, and we can feel invaluable, unheard, and misunderstood.

If our partner has poor communication skills, we may feel anxious and frustrated because they do not understand what we're trying to tell them. We may feel like the conversation isn't going anywhere and we're speaking to a brick wall.

It is important we recognize when we lack communication skills and come up with effective solutions that will help us (and others) grow so we can have healthier long-term relationships.

Poor Communication: What to Look For

Here are a few signs that I encourage you to keep an eye out for. When you notice them in yourself or in others, you can do your diligence and work to rectify them.

Shutting Down

Let's say you're speaking with someone and they're not saying a word. Instead, they're staring at you blankly and staying quiet. When you notice this, try different ways to engage in conversation with them—ask them questions about the topic and ask them their thoughts to demonstrate you care about what they have to say.

If you are the one shutting down, find out why. Is it because the speaker doesn't stop talking? Do you feel offended or triggered and prefer to keep quiet to avoid confrontation? Understand why you shut down so you can find ways to rectify your behavior and have more effective conversations.

BottlingThingsUp

It's never a good thing to keep things inside, especially when you have a lot to say. It actually creates more of a mess than we realize. When things become too difficult to handle, we will blow up, and everything we want to say gets thrown at the first person within earshot. More often than not, the person that witnesses our explosion doesn't have anything to do with why we're triggered—they were just unlucky to be near us when we blew up.

ScreamingYourLungsOut

Poor communication skills can result in a lack of emotional management. Since we don't know how to express ourselves when verbally communicating, we tend to lash out in anger and frustration. Our emotions feel out of control, and in order to try and control them, we divert to yelling.

Doing this actually makes things worse. Animosity is heightened, no one wants to be around each other, everybody gives each other the silent treatment, and there are no resolutions. This type of behavior can destroy relationships and worsens our communication skills.

ExperiencingAbuse

When we are reactive communicators, abuse may come into play. We may say things we don't mean in order to hurt the other person, which is verbal abuse. We may hit them or be hit back to demonstrate physical strength, which is physical or domestic abuse. Or we may experience being in the presence of a narcissist, who takes advantage of our emotions for their own benefit, which is emotional or psychological abuse.

When we have poor communication skills or we speak with those that do, the lack of emotional management can lead to a form of abuse without realizing it. It can greatly affect our mental health and make us feel unworthy, which can result in severe anxiety, depression, or stress.

LackofClarity

We can experience a lack of clarity in a variety of areas. We don't know what we want or need, our expectations are not clear to the other party, and we don't know how to clearly express what we're looking for to our team.

Lack of clarity can make people frustrated, annoyed, and upset. It can make them (and us) feel confused, lost, overwhelmed, and stagnant, which can make us feel underproductive and lack efficiency in achieving results. It can make us shut down and feel burned out because we don't know how to communicate the next steps or even what the next steps are. It can also make us question whether we're doing the right thing or whether the relationship is good for us.

Reasons for Your Struggles

Sometimes, communication can feel difficult. Why is that? There are a few reasons why it can feel like a challenge:

First, we have different communication styles. We all speak in unique ways—usually, this is based on our culture and the way we are brought up. For example, the rich and wealthy could speak in a very proper, high-class tone, whereas the average person can speak with slang, curse words, and have a very casual conversation. An average person may speak with someone of high caliber but will experience challenges because they're not speaking with them the way the other party is used to. This can lead to misunderstandings, lack of disrespect, and feeling offended.

We may also be someone (or engage with someone) who exhibits a demeaning attitude. It would feel difficult to speak with them because we feel as if they're talking down to us, and that doesn't feel good by any means. Our self-esteem and confidence can take a hit, and we will feel disempowered. It can cause us to lose trust and respect for the person and, more than likely, let go of the relationship because it feels toxic.

Why Social Anxiety?

Social anxiety affects about 5.3 million people in the United States (WebMD, 2021). When you experience social anxiety, it's usually because it's challenging for you to speak in public or have a conversation with someone. Your hands feel sweaty, it feels like you can't breathe, and your heart races like crazy.

If you're experiencing social anxiety, it could be for a few reasons:

- Youfe el judged.
- You're embarrassed.
- Youfe el everyone you meet is secretly criticizing you.

- You're very self-conscious about people paying attention to you.

- Youfe el shy to make eye contact.

- Youhave afe ary ou'llsay the wrong things.

It is important to realize that social anxiety is a mental health disorder. It doesn't mean anything is wrong with you—there are ways to overcome feeling anxious, so social anxiety is not at anall- time high.

As someone who struggles with social anxiety, I know the feeling. I encourage you to seek professional help and use the lessons I teach in this book to help you overcome these messy feelings so you can finally increase your confidence and know how to limit the negative thoughts that show up. Chapter three will speak more about how to let go of your negative thoughts andc hallenge your inner critic.

Why Should You Talk to Anyone?

There are many benefits to talking to strangers. If you have social anxiety, you may think otherwise, but I wanted to offer you a few reasons why talking to strangers can help increase your confidence:

- Strangers can become new friends in your circle.

- Strangers can help you expand your circle. The more people you meet, the more people you can connect with.

- It's an opportunity to meet your future partner. When connecting with new people, you will find things you have in common with them, and attraction can present itself.

- Some of your greatest friends can come from talking to randompe ople.

- Talking to strangers helps you increase your confidence andhe lpsy oure lease someofy oursoc ialanxie ty.

- It's fun and exciting to learn about new people. They could be in your life for a short season or for many, many years. It's a great way to build potential life-long relationships.

When meeting new people, I always suggest keeping an open mind. Although it may feel intimidating to walk up to a random person, introduce yourself and have a conversation, it can also become very exciting. Your meeting could make for a great, intriguing story one day. Some people find their partner by chatting at the grocery store or walking their dogs at the park. Or you may meet your best friend by sharing your crayons when you were in elementary school. You really don't know who you could meet, so it is important to trust yourself and be open to the relationship. I've always believed that the universe brings people into our life for a reason, whether it's for support or to teach us a lesson. They can stay for a few months or last for several years. The relationship can blossom into something extraordinary, so even though you may be nervous, I encourage you to push your anxiety down so you can bring your bravery to the forefront, ask the universe who you should meet today, andke ep your eyes (and heart) open.

Self-Reflection Questions

To help you get to know yourself and what you're going through, I have prepared a few questions you can ask yourself. I encourage you to answer these in your journal or a notebook soy ouc anbe gint akingac tion on your own self-development:

1. Am I currently living my best life? If not, what do I need to change in order to make it happen?

2. What is my biggest struggle when it comes to communicating?

3. When I'm in the middle of a conversation, how do I feel? Am I embarrassed? Feeling judged? Nervous? Lackoft rustinmy self? Why do I feel these feelings?

4. How do I describe my communication skills when it comes to my relationships? Could they be better? How so?

5. How can I become a more effective leader at work?

6. What do I need to learn in order to become a better communicator?

7. What are some ways I can creatively express myself when I'm communicating?

8. What is the message I'm trying to portray to others? How can I become clearer so people understand what I'mt rying to say?

9. What is my #1 fear when it comes to communicating with others? What do I need to do to overcome it?

10. What are three goals that I have that will help me become better at communicating with others? What do I need to do to achieve these goals and become a better version of myself?

You should answer these reflection questions as truthfully as you can. The more honest you are with yourself, the better. Answering these questions can help you enhance your communication skills immediately. By reflecting on them and holding yourself accountable, you'll become aware of what needs to shift in order for your life to change.

The next chapter is the first step in my six-step framework. It is a powerful chapter based on self-esteem and helping you understand your core beliefs and where they come from. By embracing this chapter, you will take the steps necessary to increase your self-esteem and self-perception so you can walk intoy ourne xt conversation with confidence.

Here's to letting yourself shine.

Chapter 2:

Step One—Letting Yourself Shine

Believe in your infinite potential. Your only limitations are those you set upon yourself. –Roy T. Bennett

"Social anxiety is a crucial emotional disorder that causes many psychological and behavioral problems" (Murad, 2020).

If we were to distinguish a relationship between social anxiety and self-esteem, I would say they are not all that different. In fact, I would say they hold an "opposites attract" or "twin sibling" sort of relationship. When a person's social anxiety is high, their self-esteem is low. It makes sense, right? When you feel socially awkward in public settings, your self-esteem takes a hit. You wonder if people are looking at you and judging you. You keep thinking there's something in your teeth and that's why they're staring—or maybe your pants zipper is down and you hadn't noticed. You think of whether you're saying the right things or if you should've said something better or more intellectual. All of these scenarios greatly contribute to your self-esteem. When you're experiencing social anxiety, you experience negative emotions of embarrassment, humiliation, frustration, and lack of trust, which leads to your lack of self-esteem and confidence.

In this chapter, we'll be diving deep into the world of self-confidence. It will teach you something that I believe everyone and their grandmother should know—how to change the way you perceive yourself. If your self-perception is negative, how do you change it so that you think of yourself in a greater light soy ouc anshow upc onfidently in the world?

Afe w other things we'll be discussing are:

- the importance of self-care so you can become self-confident

- how to use your inner voice so you can show up authentically confident

- why self-esteem and poor communication skills are connected and how you can rectify both so you get the best of both worlds

- the importance of dressing up to look confident on the insideandout side

- how your body language can make a huge difference in the way you communicate non-verbally. What type of message are you sending?

- the importance of being yourself

- the importance of affirmations and how to use them to instillmore confidence

Understanding these topics will help you create a well-rounded image of yourself—one that is confident, has deep self-love, cares about themself and their well-being, knows who they are right now, and doesn't allow anything, such as social anxiety, stand in their way of becoming a greater version of themselves.

Just like chapter one, I will provide a little exercise at the end of the chapter that you can participate in so you can start acting on some of these sections immediately. This is your moment to shine—sole t's get brighter!

Your Self-Esteem Has a Say

Imagine if your self-esteem was low, and you viewed yourself in a negative way. Let's say you look in the mirror every morning and you say nothing but negative things to yourself—what can happen here? Can you trigger social anxiety? Of course, you can.

When you experience low self-esteem, you carry it with you in public settings. If you perceive yourself as someone who doesn't have anything valuable to say or you believe people won't care about what you're saying, you'll show up in a social environment with that same mentality. And boom—social anxiety begins to show itself.

In order to manage your social anxiety and increase your self-esteem, it is important that you understand how you perceive yourself so you can rectify it moving forward. If you perceive yourself negatively all the time, you can find out what triggers it and do your part in healing so it no longer runs over in social settings.

There are a few ways that come to mind when explaining how lowse lf-esteem can affect social anxiety:

Your Core Beliefs

Your core beliefs have a huge say in how your self-esteem is affected. From the time we were about five years old, we developed beliefs on how we view ourselves and the world. If someone around us makes a comment that having a business is not worth it and it will always be doomed to fail, we grow up believing that statement, regardless of whether it's false. If we are told we are too skinny, that comment will become a core belief that is ingrained in our subconscious mind, and for many years, we'll take that belief with us without realizing it. That belief becomes part of our decision-making. We'll look at ourselves in the mirror every morning and tell ourselves that we're too skinny and our clothes will never fit, and it'll make us self-conscious. What happens after that? Our self-esteem decreases little by little to the point that it makes us anxious and, eventually, depressed. But it doesn't stop there. We may decide not to leave the house in fear that people will not like the way we look, so we prefer to hide instead.

When it comes to social anxiety, our core belief system could be rooted in the fact that people made fun or laughed at us while we did a presentation at school, and that made us incredibly anxious and diminished our self-esteem. Sure, we can bounce back from feeling embarrassed, but sometimes, it can take many years to do so if we don't understand how it's affecting our self-esteem and confidence.

Where Does Low Self-Esteem Come From?

Low self-esteem can happen in almost any experience. It doesn't only take one instance; low self-esteem happens over time, and if the experiences become too repetitive and constant.

Someoft he ways that can contribute to low self-esteem are:

- being bullied, ridiculed, and made fun of at school (this is a *big* factor!)

- after traumatic experiences, such as domestic, sexual, verbal, or emotional abuse

- when elders make negative comments about what you're wearing or what you look like; they may think they're harmful, but they're, in fact, detrimental to our confidence

- constantly being criticized and compared to others.

- when we feel ignored or unworthy of attention

- when our parents have high academic expectations of us

- when our teachers or coworkers make comments that makeusfe el worthless

- the way we speak toourse lves

Low self-esteem usually begins when we are little and we find ourselvespart ofsome   (or all) of these experiences.

The Voice Within

We all have an inner voice—it helps us make decisions. I have learned that throughout my own social anxiety journey, this inner voice can either be positive or negative—sometimes, it can be both. One may tend to be louder than the other; it is up to us which voice we choose to listen to.

When we experience low self-esteem, it is obvious we are listening to our negative inner voice. The one that tells us mean things and constantly criticizes everything we say and do. I call this voice the *inner bully*. We may no longer associate with our physical bully from grade school, but our inner bully always travels the journey with us. Sometimes this voice is located deep within us, controlled and dormant, but other times, if we allow it to, it can rise to the surface and become the culprit of our negative decision-making. It can steer us away from extraordinary opportunities and make us think we will fail if we goaft er them.

When it comes to feeling socially anxious, this voice can feed into our anxiety and belittle us to the point that it makes us lack confidence in not only public settings but in all other areas of our daily life. All of a sudden, we're experiencing social anxiety at the coffee shop, at work, during family gatherings, at restaurants, at our children's basketball games, at ballet recitals, at parent-teacher interviews—the whole nine yards.

History Repeats Itself

Experiencing social anxiety and having a lack of confidence and low self-esteem is a journey that continually repeats itself over and over again like a broken record—that is, until we decide otherwise.

When we are anxious, especially in social settings, we feel constantly ridiculed, judged, and misunderstood. Once we've left the environment, we find ourselves becoming our inner bullyandw e beat ourselves up for what we did or didn't do.

Why couldn't you have been more relaxed and spoken to that person?

Ican'tbe lieve you just said that. That was stupid!

Yous houldn't have even gone to the event—what's the point?

There was no way people enjoyed your company or liked what you wore. It would'vebe en better to stay home instead.

For days, and sometimes even weeks, we will play the experience over and over again in our heads. And every time we think about it, our self-esteem continues to decrease, and before we know it, our confidence is lost, and we feel even more socially awkward. History continues to repeat itself every time we attend a social gathering and our negative thoughts never quit. It becomes a vicious cycle that we get lost in without ever finding the nearest exit.

Connection Between Self-Esteem and Poor Communication

The connection between self-esteem and poor communication is imminent. When we have low self-esteem, we struggle with communicating with others. We become shy, afraid to share our authentic voice, and instead listen to the negative voice in our head that tells us that people don't like us. In the back of our minds, we're constantly thinking, *I wonder what they think about me? Do they like me? Or do they think I'm a loser?* These questions linger every time we attempt to have conversations, and our mind searches for evidence that what we're telling ourselves is true. Due to having low self-esteem, our Reticular Activating System (RAS) is piqued, and negative thoughts linger inourmindsandaffe ct how we have conversations.

Dress to Impress

> *Simplych angingth e way you dress can have a drastic impact on how you think about yourself.*—Chloe Le vin

Every single time you choose a piece of clothing, you share a little bit of your personality. I'm sure you've heard of the term "dressing to impress?" Usually, that means dressing in a way that impresses those you meet, but in this case, I would shift this mindset to dress to impress yourself rather than focus on impressingot hers.

The way you dress silently shares how you're feeling in the moment. If you're feeling sluggish, lazy, or sick, you may opt for a loose T-shirt and baggy jogging pants. If you're feeling fantastic, you may choose a classy suit and tie or an elegant dress. In any case, it doesn't matter what you wear—you could wear jogging pants and a stained T-shirt—you can still exude confidence in the way you carry yourself. If you're walking with your head held high, regardless of the noticeable coffee stain, people will notice your confidence more than what you're wearing.

Of course, I don't suggest wearing coffee-stained clothes—it can insinuate that you're unprofessional and sloppy, but you get the point. The way you dress does matter, especially to your self-esteem. Choose clothes that fit your unique style and personality and that you feel confident in. If you feel good in what you're wearing, you will offer a great impression to others, so before you try and impress others with what you're wearing, learn to impress yourself first.

Dressing More Confidently

In order to dress more confidently, here are a few tips that I suggest:

FindYourUniqueStyle

Wear clothes that suit your personality. So often, we want to follow the clothing trends from social media influencers, but sometimes, those trends don't fit with what we're comfortable with. Just because someone says that the color orange is the color of the month does not mean you need to run to the mall and buy something orange so you can fit in. Orange may not be the right color for your skin tone; if you wear it, you may feel uncomfortableandlac kc onfidence.

Rather than follow trends from influencers, forge your own clothing path. Consider your unique style—do you love wearing ruffles and lace? Go to town with it. Do you feel confident wearing tight-fitting clothes that show off your body? Wear them. Wear clothes that not only make you feel confident but showcase your individuality and self-expression. It helps you build your confidence and enhance your self-esteem.

Only Purchase Items You Love

Chances are, you have a drawer or a closet full of clothes that you barely wear. You may have only worn them once, or the tags are still attached because you got home, tried them on again, and didn't feel right in them. Don't worry; this happens.

To avoid an excess amount of clothes that only take up space, buy items that you absolutely love. You could be at the mall and find clothing you only like, but because your partner said it looks good, you buy it. As you're getting ready for an event, you try it on, and you second-guess your purchase. It doesn't feel right; therefore, you don't feel confident, and there it goes to the bottom of your drawer, never to see the light of day again. I'm sure you can relate to this.

Purchasing items that you truly love will help you with a few things:

- save money
- ensure that you wear them again and again
- increase your confidence because you feel good wearing them
- enhances your style and personality

Feel Comfortable in What You're Wearing

Women may love the look of stiletto heels, but if they're too high, they will feel awkward wearing them. They may even stumble and fall, which doesn't exude confidence. However, they may feel more comfortable in a flat heel or a kitten heel that offers a little height but doesn't feel overwhelming to walk in.

It is always encouraged to wear clothes that you feel comfortable in. It is not encouraged to follow a crop top trend if you're uncomfortable showing your muffin top. If you follow the trend regardless of your discomfort, you'll only feel awkward and not as put together as you'd like. How can you feel confident when you feel uncomfortable with what you're wearing? This will only give you the perception that you're trying too hard to fit in, and when you don't feel good, you won't look good. Confidence always begins with how you feel internally, regardless of whether you're wearing the top-rated blouse of the season.

Dress for Your Body Type

If you're on the heavier side, you may not feel comfortable wearing tight-fitting clothes that accentuate your curves; instead, you may opt for a looser and more relaxed fit. If you have a toned and shapely body, you may enjoy a v-neck top and short skirt as a female and straight-legged jeans and buttoned-down collared shirt as a male.

Dressing for your body type will not only help you feel more confident in your skin, but your clothing will hug your curves in all the right places. If you're unsure of what your body type is, seek help from a seamstress or fashion stylist as they can guide you in the right direction and help you choose clothing that looks and feels good.

Also, don't just choose clothing that is fashionable and stylish. Although this can be a good thing, a certain type of clothing may not suit your body type. You may look stylish and hip, but on the inside, you feel silly, uncomfortable, and awkward. This can decrease your self-esteem drastically because if you feel silly, chances are, you'll think that everyone is secretly judging what you're wearing, and your confidence has gone out the window.

DressfortheOccasion

When you're getting ready for an event, it is important you mentally note what the dress code is. If you're heading to a picnic, wearing heels or other dress shoes won't be suitable. You can wear them, but you might feel a bit overdressed, so you may offer the wrong impression, which makes you feel uncomfortable.

On the other hand, if you're attending a wedding, and you choose to wear white, you may also get many criticizing looks because it's a no-no to wear white because of the bride. You could feel confident in your outfit, but the looks people offer you may drain your confidence. Paying attention to how you should dress for the occasion is important. If you're attending a fancy gala event, it is encouraged not to wear a sundress or jeans. Instead, dress to the nines.

You can feel confident in anything you wear, but taking a mental note of what the occasion is and dressing to suit it will only enhance your confidence rather than dial it down.

From Body Image to Body Language

Your body can tell the world (almost) everything they need to know about who you are. The way you present yourself, the way you sit, stand, lean, cross your arms and legs—each and every bit of your presentation can communicate a message.

You should pay attention to how you're using your body language to share a message. For example, whenever you're flirting with the opposite sex, you may lean toward them and point your feet in their direction to show your interest. A woman may flip their hair and bat their eyelids as they casually lean in closer to the man they're interested in. Every part of your body language means something when you're communicating. Body language is the non-verbal communication we spoke about in Chapterone .

Rachel Beohm says, "You use your body to communicate. How you feel about your body affects your non-verbal communication" (2018). If you don't feel confident with your body image, your body language can suffer and might give off the wrong message. Your body language might show disinterest in a job interview because you're slumped over with your arms crossed, but in reality, you're not feeling confident in the suit you're wearing, and you're beating yourself up for wearing it. All you can think of is, *What the heck was I thinking?* Because of it, you're losing focus and lacking confidence, and your body language clearly demonstrates how you're feeling. I don't know about you, but I'd be surprised if I got the job if I was in that sameposit ion.

Body Image and Social Communication

Howworth yyoufe el about how you value yourself affects the way you behave with yourself and communicate with others. –Sachchidanand R. Swami

Your body image can be a solo representation of how you communicate with others. If you feel unworthy or lack self-esteem, you may be shy when giving a presentation at work. You may hide behind your scarf or even your hair at a networking event. If you're unhappy with how you look, you feel dissatisfied and untrusting in your relationship. Jealousy and possession might ensue and can cause many difficulties when you're communicating.

Some people may not believe that how you feel about yourself makes a difference in how you communicate with others, but believe me, it does. At times, you don't even have to say anything and your body language and self-esteem say a lot. This isw hen the term "actions speak louder than words" is coined.

If you perceive yourself in a negative way, you must recognize the areas you need to work on so you can begin enhancing your self-image and confidence. If you don't like how you look in a skirt, perhaps opt for a dress or a nice pants suit instead. If you dislike the way your curves show in tight-fitting clothes, consider wearing a looser fit and clothing that gives you room to breathe and relax. Making little changes will not only enhance your self-image but can also strengthen your communication with others. When you're confident in your own body, your communication is stronger and well-received.

Improving Your Body Image

There are several steps you can take in order to improve your body image so you can feel more confident and enhance your communication skills:

Appreciate Yourself

There are many things you have accomplished—graduating from college, getting an amazing job, having a family, buying a house, launching a business, making an excellent monthly income, going on vacation—all of these things make up who you are. They make up how you choose to experience your life. Learn to appreciate yourself for all that you've done and all you continue to do so you can remind yourself just how unique you are.

Create a List

Write down a list of things you love about yourself. To be honest, this is actually one of the most humble things you can do. It may not seem like it; in fact, it may seem a bit egotistical and prideful, but when you create a list of things you love about yourself, it brings you back into a sense of humility. It reminds you how far you've come in your journey and the difficult phases of life you've gone through, so learning to enhance your body image is a piece of cake.

Learn to Accept Yourself

"Beauty is a state of mind, not a state of your body" (*10 steps to positive body image*, 2018). One of the first steps to improving your body image is learning to fully accept yourself, despite your flaws and imperfections. We can pick apart everything about us down to the tiniest thing, but that doesn't do anyone any good. It'll only make us more miserable, shy, and less confident. By learning to fully embrace ourselves, we can feel beautiful inside and out and exude a positive body image.

Control Negative Thoughts

I know this is easier said than done. Sometimes, we are not even aware of when we have negative thoughts—they just come naturally, especially when we're continually surrounded by negativity. But most often, however, we can detect the negative voices; the ones deep down within us that tell us that the outfit makes us look hideous, our makeup is horrible, or the shirt doesn't match our pants. These voices are the ones that steer us down a path of self-loathing and can be the number one culprit that diminishes our self-esteem. By learning to control these voices, you take your power back and shift your mindset so that you empower yourself rather than disempower yourself.

Create a Positive Tribe

Surround yourself with those who are full of confidence so they can rub off on you. When you surround yourself with like-minded people, their positive energy transfers into you, and you focus on being positive. It can also go the same way with negativity. If you're always hanging out with people who tear each other down and make fun of each other, their negative energy can help influence how you view and value yourself. Creating a positive tribe and surrounding yourself with people that bring value and empowerment into your life will not only help enhance your self-esteem, but their support will bring meaning to the way you perceive yourself every day. If they're always supporting you and cheering you on, you'll feel great, your confidence shows in the way you present yourself, and how you communicate will get stronger.

Being Yourself With Social Anxiety

When you have social anxiety, it can be an overwhelming and stressful journey. You don't know how to communicate with people, you feel like you're being judged and criticized all the time, you're shy and nervous, and you're always in your head. You're so wrapped up in your social anxiety… When do you ever think about being yourself? In fact, constantly paying attention to what people think about you doesn't give you much space to be the real you. You try so hard to fit in during social situations that you forget about being yourself and try to be someone you're not.

For many years, I had a lot of social anxiety. I'm still struggling with it, but I'm getting better. I was so worried about what others thought about me that I became afraid to embrace my individuality. When my kids would have playdates or birthday parties and the parents would stick around, I did what I could to fit in and engage in conversations with them. Most of the time, it didn't work—I'm sure they could tell I felt socially awkward. I worried too much about being judged, so I would dow hatIc ouldt oble ndinrat her than stand out.

In Ellen Hendrickson's book, *How to Be Yourself,* she writes: "What socially anxious people fear most is not judgment by others in and of itself, but that the judgment is right and correctly exposes their hidden flaws" (Suttie, 2018). She goes on to say, "We think there is something wrong with us, and we avoid it in order to conceal it. In our minds, if it comes to pass, we'll be rejected, humiliated, or exposed."

The moment I read about this, everything felt like it clicked. In my mind, I couldn't allow anyone to see the real me because I was nervous, scared, and lacked confidence and self-esteem, so being my true self was not going to happen. It's not that I was avoiding being myself; I was avoiding the judgmental looks I was scared to receive because I showed the real me. And because of spending so much time avoiding potentially awkward situations, I became socially awkward myself. What a ripple effect, isn't it?

So how can you be your true self when you're experiencing socialanxie ty? Here are a few ways that can help:

Shift the Way You Think

Let's face it—our minds can make us feel like a crazy mess and can produce many negative thoughts that don't serve us any good but increase our social anxiety. Most often, though, we don't even know these thoughts exist. They become so strong in our belief system that they feel natural to think about, and to us,t hat'sjust ournat uralw ay of being.

By choosing to shift the way we think and to actually be intentional with thinking differently, we can find a way to be ourselves. For example, if you find yourself thinking, *I'm going to make a fool of myself*, or *Everyone is going to judge me*, take a moment to pause and ask yourself if those thoughts are really true. More than likely, they're not. You're just preparing yourself for what can potentially happen. You're creating a scenario out of F.E.A.R.—False Evidence Appearing Real (Clark, 2020). They're nowhere near the truth, but in your mind, you've already decided they are. By shifting these thoughts, you can take back control of your life and create a different story.

You can also learn to reframe your thoughts. Instead of thinking, *Everyone is going to judge me*, reframe the thought by saying, "I'm going to show up as the real me and that's the best I can do." By making these simple changes, your mindset begins to shift in a positive way and helps you offer yourself compassion as you navigate a social situation.

Offer Yourself Compassion

When we have a social anxiety disorder, it can be a stressful and overwhelming experience if we don't learn to show self-compassion. I want you to know something: Just because having social anxiety feels uncomfortable, it doesn't mean that you need to let it control you and your behavior in social situations. You can learn to develop self-compassion to help you manage what you're going through.

When I experience social anxiety, I have trouble coping. I beat myself up for being so awkward, I don't make friends easily, and, at times, I don't feel I'm good enough. I am quite hard on myself, actually.

This is where self-compassion can strongly come into play. When we're anxious, we're hard on ourselves. We don't understand why we have to be that way, and we hold a grudge against ourselves for struggling and for having difficulty overcoming this awkward feeling. By developing self-compassion, we can come into accordance with mindfulness. Being mindful is about focusing on the present moment and what it has to offer. When we feel compassion, we acknowledge our current feelings, tell ourselves it's going to be okayande mbrace our resilience for getting through it.

It is important to remind yourself that you are doing the best that you can in these situations, and even if you feel awkward and anxious, it's okay because, every day, you're getting better. This thought process helps you become more grounded in who you are and helps you become aware of your feelings and any negative thoughts that show up. With self-compassion, beating yourself up becomes less of a ritual and is replaced with acceptance, self-trust and self-love,andc are.

Create an Action Plan

When we feel anxious in social situations, the first thing we want to do is run into a corner and hide. We do what we can to avoid being seen and called out. By creating an action plan before you arrive at the event, you can avoid your awkward exit strategies of avoiding eye contact, rehearsing your speech over and over again, and smiling and laughing like a fool at nothing because you're not sure how to get over feeling awkward. Instead, you can become aware of your regular exit strategies andfindaw ay to let them go.

For example, you can challenge yourself. If you notice you avoid eye contact a lot, challenge yourself by looking at the person directly in the eyes when engaging in conversation. It may feel awkward at first, but eventually, it will feel natural to look at them, and it will give the impression that you are listening attentively. If you find that you rehearse what you're going to say a million times over before you even arrive at the event, make a mental note to let go of rehearsing so you can learn to trust yourself and what you're going to say. This will help ease some stress and make you feel more relaxed. I can understand that you want to rehearse what you want to say so that your speech comes out perfect and intelligent, but doing this will only increase stress and overwhelm, especially when you forget what you were planning to say and draw a blank. Can we say awkward?! Create an action plan to let go of the behaviors that induce your social anxiety, and you will notice that you're less anxious and more confident as time goes by.

Put Yourself in Uncomfortable Situations

Obviously, this is easier said than done, considering most situations feel uncomfortable when you are socially anxious, butit truly helps. Here's what I mean by this.

When our social anxiety disorder is severe, we do what we can to avoid social situations as much as possible. Most of the time, we prefer to stay at home rather than put ourselves in a situation where we are anxious, but psychologically, stepping intot he lion's den can be a very good thing.

When we want to experience transformation and personal growth, discomfort is always required. Jocko Willink says this quote, which you may remember: "There is no growth in the comfort zone" (n.d.).

When we want to overcome social anxiety and become more confident with being ourselves, it is important we continue challenging ourselves and our discomfort. Rather than avoid an event just so you don't feel anxious, attend it and tell yourself everything is going to be okay. Organize playdates with your children's friends and invite the parents to stay. Intentionally engage in conversation with them rather than avoid their eyes altogether. Find a way to be yourself, even if your negative thoughts fight with you and tell you negative things in order to avoid the situation. Avoid every urge to run away. When you can do this and stick it out, you'll notice that your social anxiety begins to dissipate, and situations feel easier to overcome. If it feels better, take baby steps—being a socially awkward person myself, I always feel it's best to intentionally put my best foot forward and step into an anxious situation, regardless of my discomfort. By pushing through the barrier, we can break the wall down, trudge forward, and embrace our confidence.

Confidence Building Tips

Now that we've discussed how to be yourself when you're feeling awkward in social situations, here are a few tips that can help you increase your confidence. I encourage you to use these the next time you step into a social situation:

Accomplish What You Need to Do

When people lack confidence, it is usually because they don't follow through with their goals or daily tasks. The next time they're faced with a similar situation, they'll immediately think they're a failure because they didn't accomplish it the last time, so they lack confidence in thinking they will actually follow through this time.

Just as we spoke earlier about challenging yourself, create a list of things that you need to do. If attending a networking event is on your list, but you're trying to make up an excuse not to attend so you can avoid an awkward situation, attend anyway and push down your negative thoughts. When you're heading home, you'll feel accomplished that you were able to push past your comfort zone and embrace being yourself. When the next event happens, rather than think you're a failure for hiding, you'll feel confident in attending, and it will no longer feel awkward.

Acknowledge Your Progress

Every time you cross something off your to-do list, acknowledge what you've accomplished. Pat yourself on the back and congratulate yourself. It is important to monitor your growth so you can see how far you've come and acknowledge the journey.

When we don't have confidence, more than likely, it's because we haven't taken the time to witness our growth. The only thing we can see is that we're still lacking confidence, and we will never be able to overcome it. But, by monitoring and acknowledging our progress as we go through the journey, we will notice what it has taken us to get to where we are today, andw e can feel grateful for how much we have overcome.

You never know—a year ago, you could be struggling with looking people in the eyes and laughing awkwardly at nothing. However, now you are no longer avoiding eye contact and intentionally engaging in insightful conversation that empowers both of you. It's always the little steps. You may not have a big chunk of the pie right now, but by monitoring how far you've come, you may notice big shifts in your personal development that you never noticed before.

Have No Fear

> *Failingis n'tyoure nemy, it's fearing failure that truly cripples you.* – Frances Bridges

What I've learned about building confidence is that not a whole lot of good things come out of being safe. Sure, there will be a time when we think that being safe is the best route to go, but if we want to grow in our personal development, we need to accept courage and build resilience.

We all make mistakes—it's a natural part of being human. But when we make mistakes, we must learn from them and not allow their failure to hold us back. One of the key things that stop us from going after our dreams and building confidence and self-esteem is fearing failure. Making a mistake, failing, and then fearing we'll fail again. Fearing failure can stop us from going after so many opportunities in our lives, so we must push down our fear and become courageous in the midst of challenges. Even if we are nervous and feel scared but go after the opportunity anyway, we can strengthen our confidence and self-trust and go after what we really want.

Advocate for Yourself

No matter what, you will always be your own cheerleader. When it's you against the world, you're the only one who can stand up for yourself. When it comes to your social anxiety, many negative thoughts can come up to enhance your nerves; it is up to you to be there for yourself and self-advocate and remind yourself that you are okay. If someone is clearly making judgmental comments or criticizing you or your abilities, it is up to you to have the confidence to hold your boundaries and stand your ground. Tell them when enough is enough and walk away because you know you don't need the negative energy in your life.

We are going to have doubts all the time, especially with social anxiety. There are going to be these icky voices inside our head that tell us we'll never be able to overcome the disorder or be "normal"—it is up to us whether we allow those doubts to take control of our life or whether we push them down and decide they don't have a place in our mind.

Who Cares What They Think?

I know—this is a very overreaching statement. As someone still struggling with social anxiety, this is a difficult thing to shift, but let me tell you something: If you can overcome this mindset block, you can overcome anything.

With social anxiety, not caring what other people think is the struggle of our lives; that's literally all we care about.

What do they think about me?

Areth ey judging me right now?

Doth ey like my outfit?

Doth ey think what I said was stupid and unintelligent?

DidIs ayth e right thing?

When you continually care about what others think about what you do or don't do, it can block you from becoming your true, authentic self. You may try too hard to fit in. You listen to other's opinions about your ideas, and if they don't like them, you try to forget about them, even though you love your idea. Their comments matter more than what you think about yourself, so when you focus on this, you try to be someone else rather thanallow your true self to shine.

It's not easy to let this one go. But, if you can, you will increase your confidence. Guaranteed.

Self-Affirmations

If you've ever used self-affirmations before, you know how powerful they can be for your self-esteem and confidence. And when you can tie them to helping you overcome social anxiety, the game can change in such a positive way.

Whenever I feel down about myself or when my anxiety kicks in strongly, I write positive affirmations and repeat them to myself every day. It is amazing how quickly my outlook changes every time I say them. If you're new to affirmations, I would like to add a disclaimer: Even though you may not hear many people say it, there are both positive and negative affirmations. Be wary of how you affirms omething.

For example, if you're saying something like, "I will no longer feel unworthy," although the positive intention is there, you're actually stating a negative affirmation. When learning about affirmations, there are a couple of important things you must know:

- The subconscious mind doesn't know the difference between past, present, and future tense; it only knows the here and now.

- It doesn't know the difference between positive and negative.

When you're stating an affirmation that begins with "I will no longer" or another negative statement, the only thing the subconscious mind recognizes is what you don't want. In other words, if you're using your affirmation in a negative way, it will bringy out he thing that you want in a negative way.

Tofurt her clarify, here are a few examples:

"Inolonge rw ant to feel unworthy."

Rather than help you feel worthy, the subconscious mind will give you more evidence of why you feel unworthy.

"Idon't want to feel anxious anymore."

You may want to feel calmer, but all this affirmation is doing is sending a message to your subconscious mind that you still want to be anxious.

"Idon't want to feel judged."

This has good intentions, but saying this statement will only communicate to your subconscious that you are looking for evidence that this statement is true and you really do feel judged.

"I don't want people to criticize me."

This is a very similar statement to the previous affirmation. You're simply sending a message to your subconscious that you're seeking more evidence of feeling criticized so you can attach truth to the statement.

When it comes to affirmations, each and every word matters.

So how can you turn negative affirmations into positive ones so they make an empowering difference in your life? Here are some examples of positive affirmations based on the four statements I shared above:

- "I no longer want to feel unworthy" vs. **"Every single day, I am worthy, and It rust myself completely."**

- "I don't want to feel anxious anymore" vs. **"Every day, I feel calm and relaxed around people."**

- "I don't want to feel judged" vs. **"Every time I am at an event, I am happy to be myself, and people love my authenticity. I am free to be me all the time."**

- "I don't want people to criticize me" vs. **"My intelligence and positive self-image shine through when I am around others. I love myself, and I love, embrace and accept every part of me."**

Self-Affirmations for Boosting Confidence

To help get your affirmation journey off to a positive start, I have created several affirmations you can use.

- Ife el calm, cool, and collected in social situations.

- I believe in myself and I trust the plan the universe has forme .

- Iinst illposit ive energy wherever I go.

- I am surrounded by positive people who lift me up and inspireme .

- I embrace and accept my flaws and imperfections. They are what makes me unique.

- I accept criticism with grace, eloquence, and sophistication. Positive criticism helps me grow into a better person.

- Even though I have social anxiety, I handle myself in socialsit uationsw ith confidence and inner strength.

- I have the confidence to learn from my mistakes and use them as extraordinary lessons for personal growth.

- I have the confidence within me to keep going and pusht hroughc hallenges.

- Every time I look in the mirror, I see a confident person looking back at me.

When using affirmations, the trick is to be consistent. Saying an affirmation once will not work. Incorporate affirmations as part of your daily self-care routine. Say statements that you can personally relate to—if you keep going, you will begin to notice significant changes in your confidence. I speak from personal experience—affirmations literally have the power to change andt ransformy ourlife !

Step One Action Steps

Based on this chapter, here are a few action steps you can take soy ouc anst artbe coming more confident.

1. **Create a few affirmations for yourself and your journey.** You are welcome to use the ones I created for you, but I encourage you to create some of your own. Start with at least five and then see how you feel. Remember: With affirmations, consistency is key, so say your affirmation statements for at least 30 days. Monitor your progress from the beginning to notice the little shifts within the month.

2. **Create a list of things that you love about yourself.** As we discussed earlier in the chapter, this is not an easy task, and it can be challenging, but I encourage you to accept the challenge and get it done. Write down a few things you can appreciate yourself for. Is it being a great parent to your children? Being an excellent and hard-working employee or business owner? Graduating from university when people told you it was impossible? Standing up for yourself in awkward situations? Whatever it is, and however small it may be, it is something worth appreciating, so create a habit of celebrating yourself every single day.

I hope you enjoyed this chapter. This is the first step in helping you build your confidence and overcome social anxiety. I highly encourage you to take action on the steps I offered so you can start to see significant changes in your life.

The next chapter, *Starting From Within*, is all about rewiring negative thinking and transforming yourself from the inside out. We briefly touched on this in this chapter, but chapter three will get into more detail on how to rewire and let go of the negative thinking patterns that are holding you back and teach you how to challenge your inner critic for a better life.

Ready for the third step? Let's go.

Chapter 3:

Step Two—Starting From Within

If you will change everything will change for you. Don't wait for things to change. Change doesn't start out there, change starts within... All change starts with you. —Jim Rohn

Remember the story I shared with you in the introduction about meeting my partner's friends? We had just traveled back to England for a visit, and she arranged a meetup to reconnect. I'm not only talking about a few friends—she invited all of them! My nerves skyrocketed. I'm already not great in social situations, but now I'm meeting all of her friends in one go?! How am I ever going to get through this and cope?

Well, let me just tell you—it was not easy. Far from it, actually. I had never felt this uncomfortable in my entire life. At times, she would leave me on my own, and I didn't know what to do. I felt incredibly awkward. I wanted to make a good impression since they were her friends, but I didn't know how. I struggled with keeping a conversation going—all I kept thinking was, *I wonder what they think of me.* I even had to excuse myself to go to the bathroom multiple times because it was the only thing I could think of to get myself out of the situation.

This little story is the reason why this chapter exists. Just like me, you may find yourself in a situation where you are meeting your partner's friends for the first time, and you have no idea how to cope with all of the negative thoughts that are floating around in your head. Most of the time, they can feel overwhelming if you don't know how to control them. This chapter is about helping you rewire these icky negative thoughts so you can learn how to challenge your inner critic—orw hatIlike to call your inner bully.

When I started to put these pieces into action in my own life, I began to see real changes. Social situations started to feel a bit better and I learned how to cope and manage my anxiety. I'm still a working progress, of course, but by applying these steps to my life, I'm noticing a difference.

Negative Thoughts and Communication

We've all had those days when it feels like nothing is going right. Maybe you had a bad day at work or feel overwhelmed by all the tasks you have to do. It may be one of those days where the stress continues to pile up, and you feel like throwing in the towel, giving up, and hiding under the covers for the rest of the day. It is very easy to let your negative thoughts take over and control your every move, but did you know that these thoughts can greatly impact how you communicate with others? You may not realize it, but it is important to become aware of this. If we are able to recognize when our negative thoughts are getting in the way and blocking our path to success and connection, we can take the necessary steps to refocus our attention and be more present in our conversations.

How Are Your Negative Thoughts Holding You Back?

Here's the interesting thing about negative thoughts: They can spiral out of control if we're not careful. One negative thought can lead to another and another. Sooner or later, your mind is covered with negative thoughts, and you believe all of them to be true.

Your initial negative thoughts can begin with, *I will never be good enough.*Andt hen it can snowball from there.

Of course, I'm not good enough; I don't have enough knowledge to complete the task.

Mycoworke rs are so much smarter than me.

Am I really a good parent to my child? I don't feel like they appreciate what I do.

Chances are, my partner can find someone better. They might just be settling with me.

Why did I have to say that? That wouldn't have come out of my mouth if I wasmore inte lligent.

And the thoughts can continue rolling down the hill like there's not omorrow.

So how can you become aware of how your negative thoughts are holding you back so you can stop them in their tracks and they don't become a deeper issue? Here are a few clues to help you spot these thoughts:

- Youmake constant excuses.

- You place blame on others rather than owning up to your mistakes.

- You have difficulty trusting and believing in yourself.

- You have constant mood swings.

- You procrastinate on simple tasks and don't take action when you need to.

- You believe it's too late to achieve your dreams.

- You have a fear of failure.

- You're a pessimist, not an optimist.

- You have difficulty forgiving yourself or others.

- You look outside yourself for answers rather than look within.

- You have difficulty seeing the positive side of life.

Changing Your Negative Thoughts

There are a few different ways that will help change your negative thoughts into positive ones, but here are the most common ways:

Become Mindful

When shifting your negative thoughts, you must become aware of them in the first place. In my experience, you cannot change something if you don't acknowledge it's there.

By becoming mindful of what you're constantly thinking about, you begin to acknowledge your negative thoughts and why they are lingering. Rachel Goldman, who is a Ph.D., suggests that you "Become aware of how your thoughts are impacting your emotions and behaviors. Observe your thoughts. Ask yourself if this thought is helpful? What purpose is the thought serving you? How does the thought make you feel?" (2023).

By asking yourself these questions, you become mindful of why your negative thoughts keep showing up. Once you know, you can reframe them and let them go.

Breathe Through It and Move

When we experience negative energy, it is usually stored in our body, and that energy can turn into negative behavior, which can transfer to others. All of this negative energy can pile into stress, worry, anxiety, and fear, and every time it stacks upon each other, it makes it harder to acknowledge and let go.

Incorporating breathwork into your daily self-care routine can help you release all of the pent-up negative energy that is being stored. You can do deep breathing exercises to help you release some of that energy so you feel calmer and at peace. Staying active also helps. I have heard of many people using exercise to de-stress and calm their nervous system. More specifically, boxing is a great way to release negative energy. You not only get a great workout, but you can also transfer your negative energy into the punching bag every time you box.

Acceptance

As you become mindful of your negative thoughts, you can learn to accept and embrace them. In all reality, the reason why we have negative thoughts is usually because they are around to protect us from potential failure and disappointing outcomes, so having them is not necessarily a bad thing. They become bad when we lose control of our negative thoughts, and they control our decision-making and stop us from achieving our goals. By accepting their presence in your life, you can thank them for wanting to protect you, and remind yourself that they don't control your life.

How to Stop Your Negative Thoughts

Stopping your negative thoughts is not an easy task, especially if you are not even aware they are there. As I briefly spoke about in chapter two, most of the time, your negative thoughts come naturally because they've been around for a long time, lingering in the background. They are around to protect you from any potential negative outcomes, mistakes, or failure, so if you're trying to stop them from showing up, chances are, you don't know how to decipher them. They can even become a habit in your daily routine.

There are a few things you can do to stop them:

Identify Them

We all have negative thoughts from time to time—it's a normal part of our personal growth. Every now and then, it's okay to have a pessimistic outlook on life—it keeps you on your toes—but when these negative thoughts become a regular occurrence, it can be difficult to stay positive and motivated. It is important to identify them. But not just identify them; challenge them so you can let them go.

Identifying them can be tricky because sometimes our negative thoughts are so ingrained in our minds that we don't even realize we have them. This is when self-awareness becomes crucial. Pay attention to your thoughts and feelings and try to identify when you have a negative thought. As you become mindful, it'll feel easier to identify a negative thought, and you can challenge it and stop it in its tracks before it becomes a deeper issue.

StopJumpingtoConclusions

Have you ever been in a situation where you heard a few facts and then jumped to a conclusion without having all the information? I know I have.

Just like when I met my partner's friends for the first time: The conversations would get really awkward, and there'd be a lot of pauses and odd looks—I automatically assumed they didn't like me, and it would make me even more nervous about speaking with them, especially since we had just met.

Assumptions are never a good thing. They can lead to disappointment, potential failure, and an overload of negative thoughts. It's so easy to jump to conclusions without having all the facts, but it's important to remember that you don't always know the whole story. It's always best to get all the information before making any assumptions. Her friends turned out to be really great people, and I realized I was all in my head and creating my own conclusions. Having negative thoughts will do this to you. When you become aware of a negative thought, rather than jump to a conclusion, challenge it and ask yourself if this negative thought is false or factual. Chances are, it's false, and you're simply making an assumption in order to avoid potential hurt.

LetGoofCatastrophizing

When we have negative thoughts, we will think about the worst possible outcome. It's a little funny when you think of it—we make up so many stories in our head as to why we're not getting that job or why our friend canceled our dinner plans... before knowing all of the facts.

They probably didn't like the way I answered the questions in the interview.

MaybeIdon'th ave enough knowledge or expertise.

Iwonde rifmyfrie ndis madatme .Wh atdidIdowron g?

AmInotagre atfrie ndtoh angoutwith ?Maybe I'mb oring.

Does it make us feel better to catastrophize? Maybe for a time, but all this does is create more negative thoughts, which create adominoe ffect on our self-esteem and confidence.

To be frank, catastrophizing is a waste of time and energy. It feeds into your negative energy and helps you jump to more conclusions, which can stop you from reaching success. Instead, focus on positive solutions and get to know all the facts first, and then make your conclusion from there.

Avoid"Should"Statements

When negative thoughts show up, it's usually because we have a *should*st atement attached to it that makes us feel worse.

Is hould've done that.

Is hould've been more talkative.

Is hould've tried harder in the relationship.

I should've gone to that event.

These *should* statements don't do anything for our positivity. Instead, they create more havoc in our minds and make us feel bad about what we did or didn't do, which creates more negative thoughts.

Become aware of what *should* statements you're using in your life and reframe them. Instead of saying, "I should've," reframe it by saying something like, "I didn't do that because I realized it was not a good thing for my life." By reframing the statement into a positive, you offer yourself compassion and help your mindfe el more at ease.

StopTakingThingsPersonally

When we have negative thoughts, we are more sensitive than usual. If someone tells us something, we immediately think they are attacking us and trying to make us feel bad. Chances are, that wasn't their intention, but we will experience negative thoughts and emotions that make us feel it was.

This is a great example about jumping to conclusions. Rather than automatically assume they are attacking you, have a diplomatic conversation where all the facts get laid out. That way, you're not taking it personally and feeding into your negative thoughts that it's all your fault and feeling unnecessary guiltandshame be cause of it.

Overcoming Negative Thought Patterns

So how can you overcome negative thought patterns so they don'thappe nagain?The re are a few ways that will help:

Journal

Discuss them with yourself. In my experience, journaling is a powerful way to let go of what is holding you back. Write down your negative thoughts and understand where the patterns come from and what you need to do to let it go.

Make it a point to journal every day. Anytime you have a negative thought, write it down and analyze it. I have found that by acknowledging them, you can accept and embrace them, and it will feel easier to let them go when they show up again. Over time, you may not even need your journal to identify where they come from—but in the beginning, journaling will help you release the negative energy and understandw here your mind's at at the same time.

BecomeYourBestFriend

We all have a friend that is always there for us. They listen when we need to vent and they give advice when it's required. We can be that friend to ourselves. Whenever we experience a negative thought, we can overcome it by listening to ourselves andoffe ringse lf-compassion.

If you need to vent to yourself, do it. It may sound a bit silly, but look in the mirror when you speak to yourself. It's as if you're speaking to someone else when you can look at yourself directly. Have a conversation with yourself just as you would with your best friend. Tell yourself what's going on. Share how you're feeling. The great thing about being your own best friend is that you will never judge or criticize yourself when you're expressing how you're feeling. You are the only one that can truly understand exactly what you're going through—take advantageofy ourow nfrie ndship.

Find Things You Can Appreciate

At times, when we are being controlled by our negative thoughts, it's because we lack gratitude. We forget about what we have in our lives that we love and enjoy. It is important to get back to gratitude and appreciate the blessings in your life.

There is always a silver lining in everything—the trick is to find it, capture it, and hold onto it. For example, if you're really nervous about your upcoming presentation at work, learn to appreciate what got you up on that stage. Enjoy the coffee that is being poured in the venue. Feel appreciative and grateful for the support of your friends, family, and coworkers. Once you build an attitude of gratitude and appreciate the little things in your life, the negative thoughts will feel obsolete and minuscule.

Stop Paying Attention to Negative Media

What creates negative thoughts quicker? Watching the news and giving your energy to the media. It's great to know what's going on in the world, but if you're constantly focusing on what's happening on the news, you're feeding your negative thoughts. I'm sure you know many people who wake up in the morning, and the first thing they do is turn on the news. Or maybe this is even you. They drive to work and listen to a radio station that talks about how backed up the traffic is. They get home and turn on the news. Their energy is being drained by sources who always share negativity. More than likely, they are always worried, stressed, and living in fear.

One of the simple and immediate things you can do to overcome negative thoughts is to turn off the TV and radio. Stop scrolling social media and reading horrible media stories or listening to the news every chance you get. Instead, find stories that empower and inspire you to become a better person. That will feed more positive energy into your life rather than paying attention to all the car accidents in your city.

The Inner Voice

Good Therapy notes the inner critic as "the inner voice that judges, criticizes, or demeans you. A highly active inner critic can take a toll on your emotional well-being and self-esteem" (2015).

Your inner critic is the inner bully that we've spoken about in various parts of this book. It feeds our negative thoughts and can diminish our self-esteem and confidence in an instant if we don't learn to control it.

Here are some examples of our inner critic at work:

I'm so fat.

I look ugly.

Why do I have so much acne?

Why don't I have a partner yet? Probably because I'm not pretty or handsome.

Why do my eyes look like that?

Our inner critic critiques every single thing about us. It can also criticize our accomplishments (or lack thereof):

You're not smart or intelligent enough.

You didn't get that job because you sucked at the interview.

That date didn't go well because you were too much like yourself.

68

You should've gone back to school... you probably would be a lot further ahead than you are now if you did.

You will never amount to anything and no one will ever like and appreciate you.

Our inner voice can tell us so many mean things that can diminish our self-confidence and the way we value ourselves—it is up to us whether we choose to listen or shut it down. It can also challenge our resilience, perseverance, and determination. When we are facing our inner voice, we can choose to befriend it or allow it to continue controlling the decisions that we make.

Befriending Your Inner Critic

How can you befriend your inner critic? It is not impossible. Here are a few ways:

Let Go of Imposter Syndrome

Imposter syndrome is when you have difficulty acknowledging your accomplishments, intelligence, expertise, skills, and talents (*What Is Imposter Syndrome And How To Overcome It*, 2023). When you feel like an imposter, you constantly doubt yourself. You feel that everyone has better skills than you or they are more talented and knowledgeable.

Chances are, these doubts come from your inner critic. You can befriend it by learning to let go of feeling like an imposter and believing in yourself. When you hear these doubts, you can thank them for trying to protect you and hold your boundaries while reminding yourself of the good you can offer the world because of how much you have accomplished.

ShifttoWisdom

Although your inner critic is around to criticize and judge you, what if you were to reframe the meaning? In other words, what if, instead of feeling criticized, you understand the wisdom behind what your inner voice is trying to tell you?

Instead of listening to your feelings of unworthiness, shift to believing that those feelings are there because you're learning more about yourself. They are there because they are helping you create a deeper relationship with your self-love. When you find a way to reframe negative criticism into positive criticism, you will hear less of your negative inner voice and more of the innervoic e that is meant to empower you.

LabelWhatYouFeel

This is where mindfulness becomes important. In my experience, there are two voices in our heads: One is our best friend that supports us and cheers us on, and the other is our inner critic. Although there are two voices, there is always one that is leading your decision-making. The trick is to become aware of which one is leading it right now.

So how can you determine this? By being mindful of how you're feeling in the moment and giving it a label. For example, if you're feeling a bit sad, take a moment to acknowledge your sadness and any negative thoughts that come with it. You know in that moment that it's your inner critic that's leading the way. If you're feeling ecstatic about something, you know that your inner cheerleader is calling the shots. By taking some time to label how you're feeling, you can determine who is leading the way the most, and if it's your inner critic, you can use your innerc heerleader's voice to shut it down.

SingandDanceAround

This is no joke. If you put on your favorite song and dance around your house, it immediately puts you in a good mood. You shift into a positive gear rather than continue to listen to what your inner critic has to say.

One of my favorite songs for this exercise is *Happy* by Pharrell Williams. Every time I hear this song, I just want to get up, dance and sing my heart out. It's a happy, upbeat song and just gets your energy pumping, even if you were sad a few moments before. This is a great way to befriend and challenge your inner critic. Their voice may be strong, but your authentic happiness andposit ive energy are stronger.

UseAffirmations

As we spoke about in Chapter 2, affirmations are positive statements that can change the entire trajectory of your life and transform it in a way that you never thought possible. By creating positive statements, you can befriend your inner critic andc hallenge them to think differently.

For example, if you always think that everyone in your class is smarter than you, that's your inner critic talking. What if you shifted this statement into a positive one and challenged the negative connotation? Instead of telling yourself, "Everyone in my class is so much smarter than me," change it to, "I am a smart, intelligent human being who knows what they're talking about. I have so much to offer the world." Can you feel the difference between the two statements? Making these slight shifts in the way you speak to yourself can make a world of difference to your self-esteem and confidence.

FindaBalanceWithAcceptance

We always seek to improve our personal growth. Rather than tell ourselves constantly mean things that don't do anything for our self-esteem but diminish it, remind yourself that you are a working progress. You are always working to grow into a better individual and it's okay that you're imperfect. This is the thing—it is important to accept and embrace your imperfections. Just because you have them does not make you weak; it only reminds you that you are a unique individual.

It is important to find a balance that will help up-level your confidence. It's okay to be shy in social situations, especially if you struggle with social anxiety—learn to accept it and then remind yourself that you are getting better every single day. You may not be great at a particular support—accept that you're still learning and decide that, with practice, you will get better over time.

Self-Care for Self-Confidence

Self-care is a concept lost on many of us, especially if we struggle with low self-esteem. We neglect it because we focus on putting others first so they can like us and have good things to say about us. When we have low self-esteem, that's generally all we care about—what they think about us. We don't think about prioritizing ourselves because, to us, that's considered selfish, but here's the thing—if we want people to care about us,w e need to care for ourselves first.

Obviously, this is not an easy thing to do. We get so busy with our personal and professional lives that taking care of ourselves first is not a priority, but I want to share something with you that puts this into perspective: If you get sick, how will you be able to take care of others? And most importantly, who will take care of you? We must learn to take care of ourselves first and make ourselves a priority so we can increase our overall well-being, which in turn, increases our self-esteem and confidence. If we don't, it can result in depression, sadness, shame,guilt ,andc hronicst ress.

There are a few ways you can incorporate an enjoyable self-care routineint oy ourdaily life style:

Talking to Yourself Positively

We've all heard the phrase "You are your own worst enemy" – this is so true. Just as we spoke about in the previous section, we can be our own worst critics, and the things we say to ourselvesc anhave ahuge impac t on our mental health and take a toll on our confidence and body image. This is when positive self-talk is so important.

When I was going through a difficult time with social anxiety, I found myself constantly berating myself and telling myself I was an idiot. I constantly self-affirmed that no one liked me and everyone was judging me. I told myself that I was not great at keeping conversations going and I would never be able to master it. This type of talk diminished my self-esteem quicker than tying my shoes. Talking to ourselves in a positive way instead of listening to our inner critic can help with a variety of things:

- reduce stress
- boostourc onfidence and self-esteem
- become more resilient to challenges
- create better relationships

- overcome fear and anxiety
- let go and forgive our past
- trust and believe in ourselves more
- combat and overcome depression

Positive self-talk can also help us manage our emotions. Instead of feeling overwhelmed and burned out, we can use positive self-talk to help us stay grounded and focused. We are no longer thinking about the negative outcome, but instead, we are focusing on achieving positive solutions. Positive self-talk can also help us become more determined to achieve our goals while reminding us that we are strong and capable and that we can handle any challenges that come our way.

Eating Healthy

Having healthy nutrition can benefit not only your body but your mind and spirit as well. When you eat healthy, you feel great in your body; therefore, you think positive thoughts. You don't feel frumpy or overweight; instead, you feel energized and fullofvit ality.

Here's a disclaimer I'd like to put out there about this: Weight loss doesn't need to be the only goal in order to have healthy nutrition. Your goals can be super simple: Increasing your energy, eating better so you can feel confident in your body, feel less tired, or have a more positive mindset. You're choosing to do something great for yourself; therefore, your self-esteem increases, and you gain confidence in your own skin. This is the only reason you need that can help keep you motivated.

Getting Enough Sleep

Your sleep hygiene can affect how you function during the day, which can increase or decrease your self-esteem. When you're overly tired, you can go about your day feeling like a zombie and not think straight. Lack of sleep can destroy your confidence because you're too tired to put yourself together in the morning. Doing makeup feels like a chore, and believe it or not,sodoe sshow ering.

When you don't have enough energy to complete specific tasks such as these, your self-esteem can lower and make you feel more anxious in social settings. Not getting enough sleep can make you feel unproductive at work or when you're cleaning the house. You lack concentration or you've had too much caffeine. You've heard of a sugar rush? Well, there is also something called a *sugar crash*. This is when you drink too much caffeine, and eventually, it hits you and makes you feel even more exhausted than before the cup of coffee. It becomes a bit of a vicious cycle—when you're exhausted, you have a ton of coffee to help keep you awake and focused. For a time, you experience a sugar rush and feel full of energy; then, as the day goes on, a sugar crash hits you. You become more exhausted to the point that you can no longer focus, and all you want to do is sleep. And then what do you do? Chances are, you'll reach foranot her cup of coffee.

Having at least seven to eight hours of sleep every night is important. Depending on your age, you can also get away with six hours and wake up feeling refreshed, energetic, and rejuvenated. When you wake up full of positive energy from the beginning, you feel confident, your self-esteem is high, and you feel energized to take on any challenges that come your way.

Maintain a Workout Schedule

Due to unpopular belief, working out is not just about having a beach-ready body or building muscle. I believe that working out your body has everything to do with increasing your self-confidence and energy. Sure, when you work out, you strengthen and tone your muscles, but you also create a body you can be proud of taking care of.

Every time you exercise, you build strength, endurance, and stamina, which greatly helps with increasing your energy and vitality. It also helps you focus more on your tasks so you can rest in confidence knowing you accomplished your goals.

When choosing to stay active regularly by going to the gym, create a consistent workout schedule so you can stay motivated. It not only helps you see results faster, but it also helps you holdy ourselfac countable for what you say you are going to do.

There is no doubt that regular exercise can help you stay focused and determined, but it can also offer huge health benefits that will benefit you in the long run:

- You can run around with your grandchildren without getting tired easily.

- You look and feel amazing, which gives you an excellent boost in confidence.

- Youfe el less tired, so you can do the things you enjoy.

- You have more energy to remain focused on your daily tasks.

- You maintain a positive mindset because you have been able to improve the way you perceive yourself.

- When you look in the mirror, you can't help but smile and love your body image.

- The relationship you have with yourself becomes deeper and more profound.

Have Fun

It is so important to have fun, no matter what your daily routine consists of. It's a known fact that when you are happy, you maintain a positive mindset. When you are positive, you boost your self-esteem, and you feel motivated, inspired, and dedicated to achieving your goals.

Having a positive mindset is a huge confidence booster, so if you want to stay in positive energy, you must remember to have fun in whatever you are doing.

There are a variety of ways you can have fun during your day:

- watch a funny movie

- go for coffee or lunch with friends

- go to the theater

- go on a date with your partner

- go ice skating or rollerblading

- go for a hike

- go for ice cream

- play your favorite board games

- take a creative arts class
- sign up for a cooking or baking class
- sign up for exercise classes
- play sports
- go to a concert
- dance around your house
- play with your kids
- learn something new
- meditate
- go for a walk in the park
- go shopping with friends
- go swimming at the beach or the local pool
- take a road trip
- go to an amusement park

There is no limit to what you can do in order to enjoy yourself. When you're having fun, you forget about daily stress and worry, and you focus on enjoying the moment. When you remain present, away from life's distractions, it's an automatic increase to your self-esteem and confidence.

78

Laugh

There is nothing in the world so irresistibly contagious as laughter and good humor. –Charles Dickens

You've heard of the infamous saying: "Laughter is the best medicine?" This phrase could go well if you were to replace medicine with low self-esteem and say something like, "Laughter is the best for low self-esteem" or "Laughter is the best medicine for low self-esteem."

Either way you have it, laughter is an excellent anecdote if you feel unmotivated, stressed, anxious, or depressed. Do you remember when you were a kid? You would be goofing off with your friends, playfully pushing them around, and laughing your faces off. All of a sudden, the horseplay gets too rough, and you fall down and hurt yourself. You may have cried for a few seconds, or you picked yourself up, dusted yourself off, and continued to laugh and joke around. As a kid, you had all the confidence in the world. Nothing in the world can stop you—you continue to laugh at the simplest things. Life was simpleandple asurable,andy oufe lt unstoppable and confident.

Imagine being a kid now. We get so wrapped up in the hustle and bustle of day-to-day life, which can be energy-draining, stressful, and worrisome. At times, we forget to laugh and have fun. Imagine if we were a kid again—what would we be doing? Probably laughing and joking around with our friends and siblingsw hile taking the day how it's meant to happen.

One of the challenges, though, is to be able to laugh at ourselves. If our confidence is low, we struggle with being able to laugh at ourselves when we make silly mistakes. Instead, we beat ourselves up and become our inner bully, which makes us feel more shame, guilt, and self-loathing. It's okay to laugh at yourself from time to time. It lightens your mood and helps you feel more relaxed, and reminds you that you are only human. It reminds you that you don't need to be perfect to succeed—you can live your life imperfectly while making a ton ofmist akesandst illfe el confident at the same time.

Creativity Is Key

As an artist, you may start your journey without having a single idea of how to draw or paint a flower. In the beginning, it may look like nothing, but if you keep practicing every day, you will eventually be able to paint an entire garden. Confidence and self-esteem build over time. It is not an overnight success. It takes effort, dedication, and consistency to increase your confidence. Expressing your creativity and developing a daily routine around it will help you enhance your confidence little by little until you get to the point where you're rocking your uniqueness.

Someoft he benefits of being creative include:

- **Being able to create a safe space that helps express your individuality, your thoughts, and your feelings.** You can journal, paint, or draw. Each creative piece, whether it's a journal entry or something else, represents who you are and what your dreams are made of. You're able to express your uniqueness and feel confident knowing that you have the creative freedom to do whatever you want to do without feeling judged or ridiculed by others. If you're journaling, this is your time to express your thoughts and feelings and be completely authentic and honest with yourself.

- **Being able to voice your opinion and share your creativity with the world.** It is important you practice self-expression, and by creating an art piece, you can demonstrate it successfully. For example, if there's a charitable cause that you relate to, you can use your creativity to help spread awareness and share your thoughts on why it's important to you.

- **Being confident in your vision.** When we're creative, we have a huge vision inside of us that is dying to be let out. By enhancing our self-expression, we turn our vision into reality, and it feels even closer now that it's out on paper. When our vision manifests, we feel confident knowing that what we set our mind to we've achieved.

Smiling as a Positive Attitude

Smiling at someone can literally change their life. We never know what's going on in a person's mind when we flash our smiles at them. They could be depressed or feeling suicidal, and we would have no idea, but smiling at them can save their life and show them that there's someone out there that cares about them.

There's also something that I call, *Smiling for Positivity*. If you're feeling down and your anxiety is making you feel more overwhelmed than usual, try smiling at yourself. I'm not kidding—this actually helps. I believe that you can overcome any negative day by simply smiling. Even if you don't feel like it, I encourage you to try it sometime, especially when your negative self-talk feels overpowering, and you're not sure how to cope. Look in the mirror and flash your smile at yourself. I guarantee your attitude at that moment will change. You'll either burst out laughing because you feel like a complete idiot, smiling at yourself randomly. Or you'll feel 100 times better and more positive about the rest of the day. Either way, your attitude will change for the better.

Benefits to Smiling

Therear e many benefits to smiling. Here are a few:

- It can help you live a longer life.

- It can help you relieve stress.

- It enhances your mood, even if you've been feeling negative all day.

- It is contagious. When you smile at someone, watch them smile back at you. Smiling can cause a positive ripple effect in the room that you're in.

- It can help lower your blood pressure. When we have high blood pressure, it is usually because we are stressed or worried about something. By smiling, we can ease ourst ress and feel more calm and peaceful.

- You are more attractive. When you smile, it brightens up your entire face, so it helps enhance your true beauty andc haracter.

- It gives you a positive mental attitude for success. When you smile, you feel happy. When you're happy, you are optimistic about achieving success.

What I've learned is that smiling is the way we express ourselves every day. It enhances our self-expression and helps us become creative with our personality and character. In my experience, people gravitate to others who are genuinely happy andsmile oft en.

In Chapter two, I spoke about creating a positive tribe of like-minded people that can help influence and empower you.

When you smile, you spread positivity and joy; therefore, you begin creating a tribe of people who want to stay in your positive energy all the time. If you were always frowning and angry, would people want to be around you? Chances are, probably not. By using your smile as part of your mental attitude, you can begin shaping your positivity and share your happinessw ith those who feel the same way.

Self-Affirmations for Positive Thinking

To sum up this chapter, here are a few affirmations that you can take with you that will help you enhance your communication skills, challenge your inner critic and start thinking positively.

- I feel at peace, knowing I am communicating effectively.

- Every day, I am strengthening my communication skills.

- Every time I smile at someone, it helps change their life.

- Every time I smile, people find me magnetic.

- My inner cheerleader is always leading the way when I makede cisions.

- Every word that comes out of my mouth is empowering and inspiring.

- Ihave funt akingc areofmy body andst aying active.

- Iamable to communicate clearly and effectively.

- Every day, I am creating a positive team of like-minded people around me. They challenge me to become better. I am so grateful to have them in my life.

- Every day, I am finding balance in my life and accepting things as they come. Whatever is meant to be, shall be.

Step Two Action Steps

For this chapter, here are the action steps I'd like you to accomplish to help you instill what you've learned:

1. **Create a self-care routine if you don't have one.** If you do, incorporate a new task to keep your routine fresh and exciting. For example, if you're already staying active by working out at the gym, incorporate healthier nutrition and cut out food that doesn't stimulate your healthy energy. If you want to have a more positive mindset, read a book on personal growth. Chances are, you have one collecting dust on your bookshelf—wipe the dust off and begin reading. By incorporating simple changes such as these, you will notice positive differences in your life.

2. **Begin acknowledging and accepting your inner critic.** In your journal, write down any negative thoughts that show up. What is your inner critic trying to tell you? Once you've written them down, include why you are accepting your inner critic's messages. Is it because you're learning how to become more resilient? Is it because you are in a season of growth and challenges, and you're deciding that you're here for it all?

3. **Challenge your inner critic.** Once you've accepted that the negative thoughts are there, challenge them. Challenge the truth they hold. Is your inner critic telling you things that are false or factual? If it's false, why are you choosing to believe them? How is it serving you? Why do you believe they're factual? By challenging your negative thoughts, you can be well on your way to healing and instilling a positive mindset.

Now that you've learned how to rewire your negative thinking patterns and challenge your inner critic, it's time you learn how to make a good impression with chapter four. Having powerful conversations and allowing them to flow seamlessly takes a bit of effort. Learning how to make a good impression from the beginning will help set you up in the right direction so people automatically enjoy your company. When you know how to instill a great impression, you will feel less anxious and more confident in engaging with others.

Chapter 4:

Step Three—Making an Impression

Twoth ingsre mainirre trievable:time andafirs timpre ssion. –Cynthia Ozick

When you first meet someone, it takes about three seconds to make a good impression (Mind tools content team, n.d.). That's not very long, is it? Knowing this stat, we are reminded that every second counts, especially when we are meeting people for the very first time.

Understanding this chapter changed my life! Even though I still struggle with social anxiety at times, the content I share in this chapter has helped me build better rapport with people. To be honest, it could've been helpful when I was meeting my partner's friends for the first time in England, but in any case, it's helping me now.

Having a conversation that flows naturally can be tricky, but it doesn't have to be. When you struggle with social anxiety, it even feels like "you're a fish out of water." You feel like you're gasping for air, your hands may feel clammy, and you may be sweating profusely. How can you ever make a great first impression if this is how you feel in your body *before* you even start chatting with people? It'll feel like you're a lost cause, for sure.

But I don't want you to fret, okay? This is why I created this chapter. If you apply what you learn here, the pieces in this chapter will help you make a great first impression the next time you're at an event or when a parent wants to strike up a conversation with you during your kid's basketball game.

We'll be discussing a few points:

- the best way to strike up a conversation

- the importance of *thinking* before talking (when you learn this strategy, it will change the game for you)

- a few tips on how to start a conversation with anyone without feeling awkward and out of your element

- how to set the tone so you don't come off as weird and overwhelming to speak to

- how your tone can have a huge impact during conversations

- the best way to read other people's body language

- how to create conversations that connect with people rightofft he bat

I'm excited because this chapter will set you up for great success in your next conversation. Of course, learning these skills is only part one of the effort; part two is when you actually take action on what you learned and apply them well so your conversations are successful. Application is when your life will truly change, and before you know it, you'll become the life oft he party.

Let's dive in.

Striking a Conversation

Let me ask you something: Have you ever thought about what you were going to say before you even said it? Let's say you were in the middle of having an argument with your partner... do you always think about what you will say next before a word comes out of your mouth? Chances are, you don't. I mean, you're in the heat of the moment, your emotions are going haywire, and there's no time to really think before you speak.

Well, here's what happens if you don't:

- Youmight say some thing you didn't mean to say.

- Youmay re gret saying what comes out of your mouth.

- You might allow your emotions to run your conversations—that is not necessarily a good thing.

- You might say something offensive and rude that could hurtot her people without realizing what you said.

Not thinking before you speak could be detrimental not only to your relationships but it could diminish your self-esteem and confidence. When we seem to always say the wrong thing or things that we end up regretting, we lose the confidence to say anything at all. We prefer to stay quiet and not speak up because our inner critic tells us it's better that way; otherwise, we might say something inappropriate again.

If you're in this boat, how can you ever share the message you want to share with others if you hide your voice in fear?

This is why it's really important to T.H.I.N.K. before you speak:

1. T -isit **T**rue?
2. H -isit **H**elpful?
3. I- isit **I**nspiring?
4. N- isit **N**ecessary?
5. K -isit **K**ind?

Is It True?

A lot of the time, just to be part of a conversation, people will over-exaggerate or say things that are not actually true. They may say little white lies just so they can get their point across and make their story more plausible and exciting. At times, they don't even realize they're saying them—it just comes out and they realize it after.

Understanding if the statement is true is the first step in this conversation strategy. Before you say something, ask yourself: Is what I'm saying actually true? Or am I stretching the truth so that I look good in front of others? In our mind, we may think it's true, but after we say it, we second guess whether it's fact or fiction.

Here's the thing I want you to remember about this: When you continually share little white lies or say things that are not true just so your story can feel more exciting, it will eventually come back to you. When people say lie after lie in their stories, eventually, they'll forget what lie they told, and then sooner or later, the truth will come out that what they said wasn't factual. In this moment and moments following, they'll be untrustworthy and inconsistent and may lose great relationships because of it.

One of the main things when it comes to communicating effectively is to be honest, even if the truth hurts. When you're honest from the get-go, you appear reliable, and people will feel like they can trust you. So before saying your next sentence to someone, make sure it holdst rueorre frainfromsay ingit at all.

Is It Helpful?

When having a conversation with someone, it is important to ask yourself: Is what I'm saying helpful to them? Can they take my words and use them to help change their life or someone else's?

When we don't think before we speak, we run the risk that what we say can turn someone bitter and make them feel negatively about the situation. For instance, if your best friend comes up to you and asks you for advice about whether they should break up with their partner, they're usually looking for some comfort. But if you were to say, "Yes, definitely. They're a douche, they're rude, you don't belong together, they treat you like crap, and you're a pushover when you're with them," what do you think their response will be? Chances are, they'll get super defensive and mad at you for being so blunt. Ask yourself: Was this response really helpful? My friend is coming to me, asking for advice, and all I'm doing is tearing down and insulting both them and their partner. Not only was what you said not helpful, but it made them feel worse about the situation, and it made them upset at you. Instead of asking for simple advice, the conversation went sideways in a matter of minutes!

Especially when someone is asking for your advice, it is important to truly pay attention to what you share with them. Take a pause before you speak so you can silently analyze what you're about to say and decide if it is helpful or if it will make matters worse. If it helps give someone clarity and direction or helps ease their pain, say it. But if you can see them getting upset or offensive, keep it to yourself or restructure your words sot hat they become helpful rather than offensive.

Is It Inspiring?

Being inspiring doesn't mean you have to be positive all the time. I mean, we're only human—we make mistakes and fail at times, and that's okay. But when you're having a conversation with someone or speaking to an audience, ask yourself: Is what I'm saying or about to say inspiring? Will it help push and motivate them into action so they can become better versions oft hemselves?

Asking yourself this question every time you have a conversation will help build stronger rapport and longer relationships with others. People love to be motivated—it energizes them into action and makes them want to become better. But what happens if everything you say berates, degrades, or ridicules them? Would that empower or disempower them? Chances are, they will feel worse about themselves, misunderstood and judged, and lose their confidence.

I believe it is our mission on this earth to do what we can to make the world a better place. To me, that means working together so we can lift up, empower and inspire others to make changes in their life so they transform and grow into extraordinary individuals who have a purpose. But it starts with us first. How can we fulfill this mission if everything we say is judgy, condescending, and misdemeaning? Rather than make the world a better place, it will only make things worse and increase the negativity that's already on the planet.

I believe each and every one of us is supposed to inspire. We all have incredible stories within us that need to be shared—the only thing we must do is speak from our heart, and the right people will hear and understand our message, and they will do their part to transform. So before you have your next conversation, make sure that what you say will inspire and empower them to make a change for the better or, at the very least, plant an inspiring seed into the next person's life so the ripple effect continues beyond your conversation.

Is It Necessary?

Here's the thing about having meaningful and effective conversations: We need to make sure that what we're saying is necessary or irrelevant to the conversation.

For example, if we're talking to our children about stealing, we must ask ourselves: "Will what I tell them add value to their lives? Or is it unnecessary and irrelevant to the conversation?" If you're simply telling your kids, "You're not supposed to steal because it's a bad thing to do," is that really adding value to their lives? Is that response helping them grow into better individuals? There is absolutely no explanation, so the response feels unnecessary. They'll just do it again. But if you were to offer a heartfelt explanation as to why it's not nice to steal and even offer a mini story so that it shows you're speaking from personal experience, that adds more value to their lives, and they will understand where you're coming from and think twice before they steal again.

So for your conversations to have meaning and substance in them rather than appear boring, it is important to understand what value you are bringing to the table that will help give them the clarity they need. It is also important to understand that even though what you're saying is truthful, it could be hurtful or break someone's heart before it is meant to be shared, so pleasebe wary of this.

This is a bit of a harsh example, but let's say you found out that your friend's partner has been unfaithful. Even though you are looking out for your friend and you care for them, sometimes it is best to keep quiet for now. It may not be the right time for them to find out, especially if it's coming from you and not directly from their partner. It will cause unnecessary animosity between all parties involved, which can destroy many relationships before it is necessary.

As you can see, there are many instances where it is important to decipher when it's the right time to say what you want to say. And if it is the right time, was it truly necessary to say right now? Or could it have waited until you were able to provide morevalue to the conversation?

These are some questions to ponder the next time you have a conversation with somebody.

Is It Kind?

Anything that we say has the power to disempower or empower others. We can say one thing, and it can truly hurt and offend people. Or we can say something else, and those words inspire people to be better. It is important we know the difference.

There's a movie that stars Eddie Murphy called, *A Thousand Words*. In this movie, the main character is a very successful book agent who is not very kind and tells lies to get ahead in his career. Eventually, he meets a potential client who notices him being unkind and sends him a gift: A Bodhi tree that contains special leaves. For every word the main character says, one of the leaves falls from the tree. The message from this movieisobvious:Choose your word carefully.

What if the words you said were attached to your own Bodhi tree? I'd imagine you'd be very careful with what you say from now on. If it doesn't have any relevance, it appears rude, or it doesn't bring any value, chances are, you wouldn't say it.

Apply the message in this movie to your own life. Every single word you say has great power—I encourage you to take this to heart so you only speak words of kindness and value rather than ignorance. So you only have empowering conversations rather than conversations that end with regret, deceit, and frustration. I know it's not always easy to think of what you're going to say before you say it, but becoming aware of what you say and if it reflects kindness will help you have more effective conversations of value and meaning rather than conversations that destroy your relationships or cause animosity.

Starting a Conversation

Starting a conversation with someone can be intimidating, especially if you suffer from social anxiety. I know this from personal experience. I used to be so nervous (at times, I still am) when I had to talk to someone new to the point that I found myself avoiding social situations altogether. Oh man, just thinking about that time when I had to meet my partner's friends for the first time… that was such a huge struggle. It made me so nervous, and my mind was going crazy with overthinking… I didn't know what to do with myself!

But I learned something through this experience. I realized the only way to overcome my social anxiety was to face it head-on. Even though it made me nervous, I started to practice small talk with strangers. I tried to strike up a conversation everywhere I went—at the grocery store with the cashier, my barista at the coffee shop, the bank teller, and parents at my kids' school—the way I saw it, this was the only way to get over feeling socially anxious and meet new people at the same time.

In the beginning, it was rather difficult. I would get so nervous that my palms would sweat and my heart would race. But I kept at it, and eventually, I started to feel more comfortable.

Here's what helped me. I'm hoping it can help you, too, and eventually, when you get more comfortable, you'll be able to have conversations with anyone anytime and anywhere you want.

Introduce Yourself

Even though technically, this should be the start of every conversation, sometimes an introduction is not the right move, but it can help. Of course, you don't want to appear silly and walk up to a random person at the grocery store and say, "Hi, my name is…" They'll simply look at you as if you're a crazy person, wondering why the heck you're speaking to them. The first thing they would think: *What does this person want from me?*

So test out your audience and notice your environment. If you're at a networking event, introducing yourself should be the first thing on your agenda. But maybe not when you're picking meat for your kid's lunches at the deli in the grocery store.

Offer Them Compliments

This is a great icebreaker. Especially if you're a female who's into fashion. To strike up a conversation with a stranger, you can compliment them on their outfit. Tell them they look nice ory oulike their shoes or purse.

96

But with this, here's a bit of a disclaimer: You must know your audience. Obviously, if you're a male complimenting another woman, they might receive the wrong message and think you were flirting with them when that was not your intention. And if they're with their partner, oh boy—you might be in for a bit oft rouble.

However, if you're a female complimenting another female on their shoes or outfit, no harm is done. You may actually even boost their confidence because of how your comment made them feel. It's easy to offer people compliments, but it is important to only do so when it's the right timing.

You can start off with, "Oh my gosh, I love your shoes. Where did you get them?" and then go from there. If they're interested in also getting to know you and having a conversation with you, they will respond with more than one answer. If not, don't take it personally and move on. They were not the right person to strike up a conversation with.

Talk About the Weather

This is another great icebreaker and can be a great conversation starter, regardless of whether you're male or female. Mentioning the weather is easy, simple, and friendly. It keeps people engaged and interested in making small talk.

I've noticed this is an effective icebreaker when you are standing in line by yourself at the grocery store. Most people waiting to pay for their items want to make small talk with someone to pass the time, so offering a comment about the weather can get an interesting conversation going. If you have social anxiety, it also helps you practice having a conversation with a random stranger so you can overcome your nerves.

Ask Open-Ended Questions

I believe this conversation starter will work if you have already built a rapport with the person or if you've coupled it with another conversational piece first. For example, if you asked them what they think of the weather and then asked them what brings them to the place, it has the potential to create a great conversation.

Asking open-ended questions is powerful, especially at networking events. There are many questions you can ask that don't only require a "yes" or "no."

"What brings you out to his event?"

"Tell me about your business."

"How long have you been doing your business?"

"What inspired you to get into the industry?"

"What type of clients are you looking for?"

All of these questions require a lengthier response; therefore, they can help keep the conversation going. The conversation will feel natural and in flow. Even if you're feeling nervous and you ask open-ended questions, you will eventually feel comfortable enough to keep the conversation going.

Ask For Help

If you're feeling stuck, you can always ask a stranger for assistance. Ask the butcher to help you find a certain type of meat, ask the grocery clerk to lead you toward the dairy section, ask the gas station attendant to give you directions to where you need to go, or ask a fellow student to lead you to your next class.

Asking for help does not mean that you're weak and unintelligent. On the contrary, asking for help can make the other person feel like they are contributing and bringing value and meaning to your life. It makes the world a better place when we always feel like we're in the place to help others as muchasw ec an.

Asking for help can also bring in a meaningful conversation. For example, if you're new to the school and you ask a fellow student to show you to the next class, you have the opportunity to chat with them and ask them how long they've been at the school and what they enjoy. At the very least, you have the potential to make a new friend.

Setting the Tone in Conversations

Maintaining a respectful tone of voice during conversations is not always easy, but it is worth the effort. It can help create a more positive atmosphere and lead to better outcomes where everyone is happy and satisfied. It can also help to de-escalate a situation and create an environment where both parties can be heard and respected. Being respectful in the way you speak to others has the power to build trust and understanding, which, int urn,inc reases rapport.

In conversations, your tone can get misinterpreted. For example, what do you automatically think when you ask your daughter a question via text, and the only thing she responds is, "k?"

Is she mad at me?

Did I do something wrong?

I wonder what's up with her. She sounds like she's annoyed about something.

For all you know, she could be very busy at work or doing homework, but her lack of response has you overthinking something that is not true. Your tone matters both in person and via text conversations. Obviously, when you're texting, you can't exactly control your tone, but you can word your sentences in a way that shows respect and satisfaction. Maybe including emojis can help to spread the appropriate reaction you're hoping for.

When you're in person, your tone matters in both your body language and the words you speak. When speaking with your partner, the two words that people usually dread is, "I'm fine" when asking how they're doing. They may not mean anything by it when they say it, but those two words insinuate annoyance, frustration, and a "Don't talk to me" kind of vibe. And when "I'm fine" is coupled with unintentional eye rolling and arms crossed in front of their chest, what else are you supposed to think? It's because of examples such as these that it is important to fully understand your tone of voice when you're engaging in conversation. You don't want to offer the wrong impression, nor do you want people to think there are hidden condescending messages behind your tone.

Condescending Tone

No one likes to feel unintelligent or like an idiot. So if you're speaking to them in a way that feels condescending, they may get defensive, annoyed, and frustrated. A condescending tone shows a "patronizing or superior attitude toward others" (Merriam-Webster, n.d.).

Afe w examples of a condescending tone are:

"You always seem to be late for everything" (You have no idea what it took for them to arrive, but you're automatically assumingt hey're irresponsible).

"It hought you knew that already?"

"Obviously,t hat'snot what I meant."

"That'snot re ally the way we do things."

"Isuppose sinc e you're new, you don't really know."

People don't really like to be around those who are condescending. It feels as though they are talking down to them, and they make them feel like they're less superior or don't know anything. It can make us lose our confidence or seem like we don't know what we're talking about.

Boredom Tone

When you're in the middle of having a conversation with someone, and you sound bored, what message do you think it gives the other person? That you don't care what they're saying. It can make the person feel frustrated and annoyed and as if they're just wasting their time speaking with you.

Your tone of voice is also not the only thing you need to watch for. You may also demonstrate boredom with your body language. Most often, non-verbal communication appears to be more powerful than actually using your voice. When your boss is giving an important presentation, and you have your head on the desk, doodling on your notepad or texting, or playing games on your phone, this does not offer the right impression. Whatdoe sy ourbosst hink?

"They obviously don't care to be here."

Because of this message, you could potentially get a warning or worse… lose your job. Exhibiting a tone of boredom may also make it feel like you're not paying attention or that what they're saying is not as valuable to the conversation as they thought it would be. When chatting with potential clients, this tone may give off that you don't care about their needs and you really dislike what you're doing. This type of energy will not land you clients; instead, it will reject them and send them to your competitor.

Supportive and Empathetic Tone

This is the tone that you want to achieve. Not only does it help bring value to the conversation, but it shows that you truly care about what the person has to say. By being supportive, you are engaging and listening intently, which can inspire the person to continue having a conversation with you.

I believe in every conversation, there are ways to show support and empathy. If the person is struggling with something, you can show support by offering them kind advice and sharing your opinion. If the person is sick, you can simply be there for them, using non-verbal communication as a means to show your love and support. If your partner has great news to share, you can match their energy and be excited with them as a way ofde monstratingt hat you support them.

A supportive tone empowers rather than disempowers. It doesn't demonstrate a condescending tone and insults their intelligence, but rather it shows that you are always there for them, regardless of what's happening in their lives. It's a very easy tone to achieve, especially when you are meeting someone for the first time. Simply cocking your head to the side and nodding is a non-verbal way of showing that you understand what they're saying and you support it. This will help you have more empowering relationships and increase the love and respect you have for others as well as the respect they have for you.

Reading Body Language

"Body language is like an iceberg. 90% of what is unsaid lies underneath the surface" (*5 Powerful Reasons Why Body Language is Important*,2021) .

Being able to read others' non-verbal communication is a superpower in itself. It's not easy, and it takes effort and awareness. Some people are very good at hiding what they're really trying to say, and others give off the vibe altogether. Reading body language can tell us a lot about how someone is feeling, even if they don't say a word.

For example, if you're talking to someone and they're slumped over with a curved back, it could show that they're bored and they don't really care what you're saying. If they are sitting straight up, it's a sign they're interested and intrigued. But, if they're smiling with their eyes, they are showing a sign that they're interested in what you're saying, and they want to learn more.

Our body language can also be used to convey our own feelings to others if we're not comfortable physically speaking about them. If we want to show someone we're interested in what they're saying, we can lean in and make eye contact. If we want to show someone we're not interested, we can cross our arms and look away or even stand up as a sign that we're done with the conversation.

Do We Really Pay Attention to Body Language?

Let's face it—we don't usually pay attention to non-verbals. Heck, we barely pay attention to our own body language and the message we're portraying with it. To be honest, we should make it a priority when we're engaging in conversation because it usually conveys the true message that we're trying to say. If we are feeling stressed or uncomfortable in a conversation, we'll probably clench our jaw and have a furrowed brow. This is a telltale sign that we are feeling anxious. Chances are, we're doing all of this without realizing we are. And if the person can read body language, this may give a message of anxiety and make the other person feel like they're saying something wrong.

They may catch you off guard and ask you if there's something wrong or if they said something to make you feel uncomfortable. That question may pose even more anxiety not just in you, but in them as well. Or, if they are enjoying the conversation, they may unintentionally copy your body language. If you cross your legs, they do the same. If you tilt your head, they'll follow suit. This is not out of annoyance but asignt hat they're enjoying the conversation.

So is it important to pay attention to our body language? Most definitely. We don't want to give off the wrong message without intentionally meaning to give it. Instead, if we learn to become aware of how we're positioning our body while having a conversation, we'll be more careful to demonstrate the right tone that doesn't offend but rather empowers.

Become Magnetic to Others

Since our body language offers over 90% of what we truly mean to say, how we present ourselves to others can have an incredible impact. We can walk into the room exuding incredible confidence, and people will gravitate toward us. We can just be standing in one corner, and we will feel magnetic to others, and they will come to us. This is not because of our pretty faces. If we're magnetic to others, it's because of the way we're using our body language.

For instance, if you walked into a networking event with your shoulders slumped over, an arched back, hair in your face, not making eye contact, and frowning, does this make you approachable? Quite the opposite, actually. It offers the message that you're bored, shy, and don't care to be there—not what you want at a networking event where you're trying to meet people who can turn into potential clients.

But, on the other hand, if you walked into the event with your head held high, smiling, back straight, making a ton of eye contact, and walking confidently, you give off the "I have to meet them" vibe. People will gravitate toward your energy because it's positive, uplifting, and confident.

If you struggle with this and you're usually the first person, I suggest practicing the *Power Pose*. You may have heard of it through various speakers such as Lisa Nichols and Tony Robbins. The power pose is something anyone can do to help instill immediate confidence before they meet people. This is great, especially if you struggle with social anxiety, such as myself.

When thinking of power posing, think of Wonder Woman or Hercules. How do they stand? Do they pose with their back arched or arms across their chest? No, they pose with their arms in a warrior pose, resting on their hips and their back straight and chest pushed out. This pose exudes confidence and esteem. Every time I do this, I get a burst of self-empowerment.

Here's a fun fact about power poses: Power poses were found to reduce cortisol by 25% and increase testosterone by 19% in aslit tle as two minutes (Van Edwards, 2021)!

If you're feeling nervous about striking up a conversation at your next meeting, I suggest you engage in a power pose for a few seconds before you head to the function. I guarantee you'll feel an immediate difference.

The Importance of Eye Contact

Eye contact can be a powerful tool for understanding what someone is thinking. Think about it. What happens when someone is feeling confident? They'll make direct eye contact and hold the stare for a few seconds. They want to make it known that they know what they're talking about. On the other hand, what happens when you're feeling anxious? You will avoid looking at the person in the eyes, and you'll look down or up at the ceiling, or your eyes will move around the room. If you're upset or frustrated, your eyebrows will arch, and you'll look at the person intensely without being the first to look away.

Eye contact is something you can take advantage of and use in a variety of areas in your life. You could be at an important business meeting, and if you want your boss to give you leadership on the next project, you'll look them in the eyes with confidence. If you are in a relationship or chatting with your partner, you'll stare at each other in a flirtatious way and not break the stare. Eye contact is an important part of non-verbal communication. When you want to say something without physically saying something, you can communicate it with your eyes. I like to think of eye contact as an unspoken language. The next time you're in a conversation, pay attention to the power of eye contact and see what you can learn.

Here are a few tips you can use to master the power of eye contact:

- **Establish eye contact before the conversation begins.** By doing this, you get their undivided attention, and then you can have an empowering conversation.

- **Establish eye contact for a few seconds at a time.** You don't want to look creepy, so look away every few seconds and then make eye contact again.

- **Try not to look away for long periods of time.** If you break eye contact for more than a few seconds, you'll appear bored or uninterested. To keep the conversation flowing, try your best to maintain eye contact as much asy ouc an.

- **If you need to look away for a second, look at another part of their face.** This will make it seem like you're still maintaining eye contact, but in reality, you're releasing a bit of discomfort.

Making a Great First Impression and Meaningful Connection

We all know the feeling of being in a room full of people and feeling like an outsider. This is your moment to make a great first impression. I get it—it can be intimidating to try to join a conversation, especially if you don't know anyone and especially if you are chocked full of social anxiety. How can you create a great first impression and meaningfully connect with others at the same time if you are feeling anxious?

Here are some tips that can help you do both:

- **Don't be late.** A pet peeve that many people have is tardiness. If you're trying to make a great first impression, being late to the event should not be on your agenda. Not only does it make you appear unreliable and irresponsible, but you wouldn't be able to connect meaningfully with others knowing you were late to the party.

- **Dress for success.** Present yourself in the best way possible. This includes not being late and looking clean cut and polished. In my opinion, the way you present yourself to others is your character resume, so you want to look as neat as possible.

- **Be yourself.** Don't try to be someone you're not. People can smell fake a mile away. Don't be afraid to share your own experiences and opinions to help build rapport and demonstrate that you understand them. This will help create a more meaningful connection and make the conversation more interesting. The best person you can be is yourself because, quite frankly, everyone else is taken.

- **Smile from ear to ear.** We spoke about the importance of smiling in Chapter three. When you smile, you look approachable and charismatic. When you walk into the room, flash your smile and people and make eye contact—this is a great way to get noticed.

- **Display confidence.** People love having conversations and hanging out with those who are confident; it shows that you know what you want and you will do anything to make it happen. Remember the power pose? This is the time to practice.

- **Engage in small talk.** Use your conversation starters as much as possible. It'll help break the ice so you can get a great conversation going.

- **Empower yourself and others.** Making a great first impression and establishing connection through your conversations is about a positive attitude. If you're feeling positive, you'll find ways to empower and compliment others. They'll see you as empathetic and supportive, w hichc anhe lpe stablish rapport.

- **Be an active listener.** A great way to establish a connection with others is by listening attentively to what they're saying. Don't just wait for your turn to talk. Listen to what the other person is saying and ask questions to continue the conversation. This will show that you're genuinely interested and that you care about what they have to say.

- **Actively engage.** Be open to the flow of the conversation. It's okay to ask questions to show your interest—people love that. You can talk to them about their interests, hobbies, and experiences. This will help you get to know them better and create a more meaningful connection. You never know—you might findt hat you have a lot in common with them.

- **Don't make this all about you.** Very similar to the last point. Go back and forth in the conversation—don't just talk about yourself. This will give the impression that you are selfish and self-involved. If they ask about you, awesome! Share a little tidbit and then bring the conversation back to them. A meaningful conversation is like a game of tennis: You serve the ball first, it bounces to your team member, and then it goes backt oy ou.That 'show you both can win the game.

Self-Affirmations to Ease Conversation Anxiety

The following are a few affirmations you can use that will help you make a great first impression, ease your stress and anxiety during conversation and establish meaningful connections:

- I am a great conversation starter.
- Meeting new people makes me feel at ease.
- I am confident with being myself.
- People are attracted to my authenticity and genuine charisma.
- I express myself in a way that is engaging, magnetic and meaningful.
- I am an extraordinary listener. People love to talk to me.
- I am confident in who I am and the message I have to share.
- Every time I walk into the room, I make an extraordinary first impression.
- My smile attracts people toward my path.
- I can flow and engage in every conversation.

Step Three Action Steps

We spoke about some very important pieces in this chapter. Here are a few exercises that will help you put these lessons intoac tion:

1. **Create a video of yourself.** Record yourself in your natural state for no more than 10 minutes. Once the video is recorded, I encourage you to watch it. The only point of this exercise is to notice your regular body language. Do you notice that you always cross your arms when you're having a conversation? Are you always slouched over in your chair? Do you not make eye contact? Do you gesture with your hands a lot? Do you notice you're always looking at your phone during conversations? This video will help you become aware of your negative body language so you can rectify it during the following conversation. For example, if you notice you have difficulty making eye contact, the next time you speak to someone, you can make it a habit to maintain eye contact. This video will help you master your own body language.

2. **This is part two of the first exercise.** Record yourself every once in a while so you can see how your body language has improved. This will help you become a master at non-verbal communication—you will notice you get better each and every time.

3. **Challenge yourself to make small talk with a stranger.** If you feel very anxious, I encourage you to push and motivate yourself to step outside your comfort zone. If you have social anxiety, this won't be an easy task, but if you can push past the barrier, you will feel more comfortable the next time.

4. **Practice your power pose.** Take a few seconds every day to step into a power pose. While in the pose, feel free to say some affirmations to help with your confidence. If you are consistent with this, you will notice that you feel more confident each and every time you have a conversation.

5. **Practice *thinking* before saying anything.** Remember T.H.I.N.K.? Actively practice it before every conversation. Notice what you're saying. Is it true? Helpful? Does it inspire and add value? Is it necessary? Are you being kind?

I hope you were able to find this chapter helpful. Making a great first impression is so important as it will help you create meaningful relationships that can last a lifetime. It'll also help you find things in common with others so you can have fun with them and enjoy the journey together.

The following chapter is about learning how to keep the conversation going. Now that you've learned how to establish rapport and create connection, you can now continue to keep it flowing, engaging and interesting. Chapter five will show you how.

Chapter 5:

Step Four—Keep It Going

Music is like having a conversation. All musicians inspire each other, and they're all geared to play something that matters.—Vince Gill

When we engage in conversation with someone, we always want it to be purposeful. A great conversation sets the tone for intention, inspiration, empowerment, and value. I have learned that knowing how to strike up a conversation with someone is one thing, but keeping it going and in flow is another. Sure, we can get comfortable starting conversations with people and making small talk, but keeping a conversation interesting is always a challenge.

First, both parties never know how to end the conversation. We're left with this awkward pause because we don't know when to cut the conversation. We keep talking and talking until there's really nothing left to say, and eventually, one of us awkwardly walks away with the other staring at the back, wondering if they were boring to talk to.

To start this chapter, here are a few tips I can share that will help keep the conversation going:

- **Don't ask yes or no questions.** Ask questions that require more than a one-word answer. This will help to keep the conversation flowing and give you more to talk about.

- **Listen and respond.** Be an active listener when having a conversation. Listen to what the other person is saying and respond with thoughtful comments. This will show that you're engaged in the conversation and will help to keep it going rather than feel boring.

- **Share stories.** Talk about something interesting that happened to you recently or something funny that happened to a friend. This will help to keep the conversation light and entertaining.

- **Ask follow-up questions.** After the other person has finished talking, ask them a few questions to get more information. This will show that you're interested in what they have to say and will help to keep them engaged.

- **Be positive.** Try to avoid negative topics as much as possible. The conversation won't feel as enjoyable if all you're talking about is war and the latest kidnapping or car accidents in the city. You don't want to be a Debbie Downer. Keep the conversation positive, light, and enjoyable.

Asking the Right Questions

John Maxwell wrote a book called *Good Leaders Ask Great Questions*. It talks about how to master the art of asking questions so you can become a phenomenal leader and become confident in your knowledge.

When you ask the right questions, it can lead to many opportunities that lead to success, building powerful relationships, and self-transformation. Asking the right questions is not just about getting to know others on a deeper level but also about getting to know yourself and building your imageandc haracter.

For instance, if you were applying for a job, what do most people ask?

"Cany out ell me more about the position?"

Theque stion is vague, common, and generic.

But what if you asked something like this instead?

"Whatdoy oue njoyabout working here?"

Sure, this question will catch the interviewer off guard and will surprise them because it's not directly about the position, but it will set you apart from the other applicants. It shows that you care about what they have to say and that you're intent on learning about the people you'll be working with. It may appear a bit unorthodox to ask this type of question in an interview, butsome times that's a good thing.

I know some people who have asked a similar question in an interview, and they got the job, so being different does work.

Asking "Why"

When asking the right questions, the most powerful questions usuallyst art with "why."

It's thought-provoking, curious, and engaging. It encourages people to offer in-depth answers rather than answers that are generic and dull.

"Whydoy oulove to do what you do?"

"Whydidy oulaunc hy ourbusine ss?"

"Whydidy oude cide to travel the world?"

"Whydoy ouw ant 6-figuresiny ourbankac count?"

"Whydoy ouw ant this job?"

Questions that start with why can introduce engaging and interesting conversations. Anytime you ask why, the conversation has the potential to continue flowing and perhaps be prone to never end, which is another issue in itself, as discussedat the beginning of the chapter.

What Happens if You're New?

If you're the "newbie" at a job, for example, asking the right questions can have its advantages and can set you apart from the others.

By asking questions, you learn more and demonstrate your curiosity. Employers love when new employees ask a ton of questions—it shows that they're eager to learn and they actually care about receiving the position and being the best that they can be.

When you're new, you welcome openness and change. You're not set in your ways like seasoned people, but instead, you're ready and willing to learn anything and everything that will help buildy ourknow ledge.

Think Outside the Box

When you're working on a project and come across an issue, asking a ton of questions can help you think outside the box. Maybe you've been working on the project for hours without a break, and your eyes are getting hazy. You can no longer think straight; therefore, clarity is lost, and your mind is drawing a blank.

What would happen if you stepped away for 20 minutes and came back to your project? Chances are, you'll have more clarity, and you'll be able to ask yourself different questions as if you're an outsider coming to help. These questions help you find the solution to your problem because your mind is now clear, and you're able to ask different questions that help you think outside the box rather than questions based on your exhaustion.

Tips to Have a Memorable Conversation

There are a few things you can do that will guarantee you have ac onversationw orthre membering:

Ask Thought-Provoking Questions

These questions will get the ball rolling. When having a conversation, you want to ask questions that get the person to think. Questions that not only require a yes or no answer but require an answer with substance.

Think of how a journalist asks questions: Their job is to get as many detailed facts as they can in order to create a compelling article that their audience will want to read. They ask their interviewees questions that get them thinking and that offer manyde tails that are substantial to the story.

When asking questions, do the same thing. And when you answer questions, follow the same model. Offer an in-depth answer that keeps the person interested and engaged so they keep asking questions. This alone will help the conversation flownic ely.

Pay Attention

The one thing that can turn a conversation sideways very quickly is when you're not paying attention. If you're asking a question and the person is giving you an answer, but you've chosen to break eye contact and text on your phone, that appears very rude and disrespectful. It can become a memorable conversation, but not the good kind.

If you want to keep people interested in speaking with you, make sure they have your full undivided attention. Put your phone away and zero in on what they're saying. The worst you can do is not pay attention to what they're saying, and then they ask you a question, and you respond with an answer that's completely irrelevant to the conversation. That feels like a slap in the face to the other person; it's disrespectful, ignorant, and can cut a conversation in half when both people are feeling awkward.

Share Personal Stories

Some of the most memorable conversations include personal stories. Of course, it is important to play this card when it's appropriate. It may not be appropriate when someone comes to you to share that their dog just died, and you speak about your own personal experience when your own dog passed. That sounds a bit self-involved and not consoling or supportive whatsoever.

Sharing personal stories, though, can show your vulnerable side and give people a taste of what your personality and character are like. It can help them relate to what you went through and, perhaps, even be inspired. I believe all stories have a brilliant message to share, so when you share a story during a conversation, you never know who it could inspire or whose lifeit could change.

Types of Questions to Ask

Asking the right questions to keep a conversation going can be tricky, but it doesn't have to feel that way. It takes a bit of strategy, effort, and wisdom on your part in order to keep your audience engaged.

There are a few strategies that you can put in place that will help you keep the conversation going so that it still feels natural:

Open-Ended Versus Closed-Ended Questions

Asking open-ended questions during conversation can be a great way to get to know someone better and build a stronger connection. It can help not only to keep the conversation going and make it more interesting, but it can get people to open up andprovide more de tailed answers.

For example, instead of asking, "Do you like to travel?" which is a closed-ended question, you could ask, "What's your favorite place you've ever traveled to?" This question offers an experience, a thought, a detailed response, or a potential memory. It becomes a memorable conversation simply because you cared enough to ask questions that help open up your audience's heart and vulnerability.

Superlative Questions

These types of questions offer descriptive words attached to them, such as best, worst, or least. They are thought-provoking and offer interest and entertainment. If played correctly, they can keep the conversation going well.

Some superlative questions include:

"What is the best vacation you've ever been on?"

"What did you love most about that vacation?"

"What is the best thing about your business?"

"What do you love most about your clients?"

"What is your least favorite thing to do during the week?"

"What do you love most about your partner?"

These types of questions not only have substance, but they offer the person's vulnerability to shine through. You have an opportunity to get to know their personality and character a little bit more, which can create a deeper relationship.

Challenging Questions

These questions help you dig deeper into a person's character. They help create a lengthier response that requires a bit of thought and perhaps self-inspiration.

Some examples of challenging questions are:

"Why do you do what you do in your business? Tell me about your why."

"What was most challenging when you launched your business?"

"What was your biggest challenge when it came to securing your first client?"

"Whydidy oufindy ourc ollege program challenging?"

"What was challenging about your job interview?"

These questions help people understand the lessons attached to how they answer. They can help a person grow into the next-level version of themselves simply by understanding what they've learned because of the challenge they experienced.

When learning to ask the right questions, remember that it can take time. Be patient and trust yourself. Don't be afraid to take a step back, relax and let the conversation flow naturally. You're not there to impress anyone, so step back and observe and allow yourself to be free to express your knowledge, wisdom, and expertise.

Active Listening

Active listening is a powerful tool that can be used in everyday conversations to help build relationships, foster understanding, and create a sense of trust. It involves listening to what someone is saying, not just hearing it, and responding in a way that shows you are engaged and interested in what they are saying.

It is an integral part of asking the right questions, so make sure you're really paying attention to the answers you're getting, and don't be afraid to ask follow-up questions. Communication is a vital skill in any setting, whether at work, at home, or in social situations. However, as we've been saying throughout this book, effectively communicating is not just about speaking; an important part is about listening intently.

In the bible, it says in James 1:19, "Be slow to speak and quick to listen" (*NIV,* 2011/1973). Listening is more than just hearing the words that someone says; it is also about understanding the meaning and intent behind them. When having a conversation, it is important to be fully present, attentive, and empathetic to the person speaking. Let's face it, we all love to talk, but it's also okay to quiet down and listen to someone else's voice for once. I'm sure you have someone in your family, or maybe your friend, who tends to chat up a storm and barely lets you get two words in. Finally, when you say something, they interrupt you and shut you down to continue talking. In my opinion, it's a bit rude and disrespectful when someone does that, but when you think about it, they're not practicing being an active listener. It's like they have to say as much as they can in a matter of minutes; otherwise, they'll forget it or miss their chance to say it. If you truly want to have an extraordinary conversation, I highly encourage you to practice active listening; otherwise, the conversation might get awkward real quick.

Active Listening Is?

According to Positive Psychology, active listening is "a way of listening that involves paying close attention to what is being said, both verbally and non-verbally" (O'Brian, 2022). When you are a master at listening intently, you pay attention to even the small stuff: Body language, the way they're presenting themselves, what they're saying, and the tone of voice. You also know how to respond so that it reflects interest, value, and inspiration. The person you're speaking to can tell that you are actively engaging with them; therefore, they feel empowered to continue talking.

Here's a fun fact: The average listener will only remember about a quarter of what was actually said during a conversation a couple of months later (Nichols & Stevens, 2014). By actively listening to the speaker, you have the potential to increase that numberandre member many of the highlights.

To be successful at active listening, there are three main components you need to focus on:

- **Listen for the overall message.** Try to pinpoint everything that is attached to the message. I'm not only referring to what they're saying but the non-verbal actions as well: the tone of voice, facial expressions, and body language. These cues can convey a deeper meaning than what they are verbally saying, and they can relay the truth of how they're feeling without physicallysay ingit .

- **Offer an emotional response.** Once the speaker is done, it's now your turn to speak. Instead of just switching the topic immediately, which is not actively listening, by the way, offer an empathetic tone. Agree with them and demonstrate that you understand what they're referring to. You can say things like, "I hear you," "I understand," or "That sounds frustrating," as these phrases will show that you're empathetic toward them and that what they're saying has a lot of value. This can help to validate and empower them in the conversation.

- **Use non-verbal communication.** Instead of only using verbal responses to express your interest in the conversation, you can take advantage of your non-verbal expressions as well. Maintain eye contact, nod in agreement, smile, laugh, lean in, cock your head to the side,e tc., as these cues will help show your interest.

As you become better at active listening, you will understand that it is different from passive listening. Passive listening is when you simply hear the words someone is saying, but you're not really giving them your undivided attention. A passive listener is the person I described above who constantly interrupts and doesn't really let you get a word in. Passive listening can make the speaker feel ignored, misunderstood, or unimportant, which doesn't make for a great conversation. In fact, the passive listener is like a one-sided conversation. However, active listeners have great conversations, and people love speaking with them. Speakers have even told them that they are fantastic listeners.

Why Is Active Listening Important?

Now that you have an idea of what active listening is and how it can play an integral part in communication, here are a few pieces I'd like to share with you about why it's so important to master, especially if you want to have great conversations:

- **Build rapport and trust with others:** You show that you care about what others have to say and that you respect their opinions and feelings. I believe active listening involves a ton of empathy and genuine concern for the well-being of the speaker; therefore, by building rapport, you can create a positive relationship with them, which helps them open up to you and become more vulnerable.

- **Helps you understand others on a deeper level:** As you're listening, you try to understand not only what they're saying but also why they are saying it and how they feel about what they're saying. This is part of the "listening for the overall message" piece of the conversation, and it can help you gain a deeper insight intot heir perspectives, motivations, needs, and goals.

- **Avoid potential misunderstandings:** If you're a passive listener, you run the risk of getting into conflict because you're not paying attention to what is being said or the meaning behind it. When you're an active listener, you can notice the overall meaning, which can help you avoid confrontation or misinterpreting what they're saying. This, in turn, can avoid potential disagreements.

- **Learn new information and skills:** When you're actively paying attention, you can notice all the little details the conversation is presenting. This is a great skill as it can help you learn new facts, ideas, insights, or techniques from others who have different knowledge ore xperience than you.

Improving Your Active Listening Skills

Active listening is a skill that can be learned and improved with practice. Clearly, it is not an overnight improvement—it takes time, patience, and determination. It also helps if you're ready to break through challenges, such as passive listening.

Here are a few tips that can help you improve so you can not onlybe agre at communicator but a great listener:

- **Be prepared.** Before engaging in a conversation, make sure that you are ready to listen actively. As you prepare for the event, decide that you're going to practice active listening. When you arrive at the event, clear your mind of any distractions, put your phone in your pocket or purse, give the speaker space to begin speaking, and set aside ample time to chat and adopt a positive attitude towards them. Show that you are curious to know what they have to say and that they have your undivided attention.

- **Keep your focus on the speaker.** Make sure that you are listening intently to the speaker and actively engaging with them. One way to do this is to maintain eye contact the whole time. It is also important to resist the urge of thinking of your own responses when they're in the middle of talking. This can make you lose your focus and make you nervous because now you don't remember what they said. When it's your turn to speak, you can focus on what you're going to say, but until then, give your full attention to the speaker and empower their need to be heard.

- **Show interest.** Remember the body language cues we spoke about? During the conversation, make sure that you show interest and actively engage with the speaker. Maintain eye contact, lean in, nod in agreement, show empathy, offer a smile, and uncross your arms—make sure the speaker is aware that you're actively listening so they can feel comfortable continuing.

- **Practice paraphrasing.** When you're engaging in the conversation, practice briefly repeating what the speaker is saying in your own words. That shows them you're listening and paying attention to what they're saying. They'll feel valued, appreciated, respected, and heard. It can also empower the speaker to keep going with the belief that they are giving you value.

- **Seek clarification.** This is very similar to paraphrasing. During the conversation, you can actively engage by asking them insightful questions in order to clarify something they're saying. This can help the conversation continue to flow at a comfortable pace.

Keep the Conversation Flowing

This is, by far, a big struggle for me. I know, probably for you too. Having social anxiety makes me feel stuck and awkward in a conversation. I never really know what to say, or I freeze up and struggle to keep the other person interested. I know I'm not the only one who's been in this mess.

I, for one, find it challenging to keep a conversation going and in flow, especially with someone I don't know well or have different background or interests—just like when I met my partner's friends (I know I keep bringing this experience up, but it's the one that stuck with me the most when it comes to experiencing challenges in conversations).

This section will help you master the art of good conversational skills. When you have phenomenal communication skills, it will help you build rapport, trust, and understanding and make you a great leader. It will also help you feel more confident, likable, and successful and will enhance your self-perception. By the end of this section, I trust you will now know how to keep a conversation going and in flow with anyone.

What Is Conversation Flow?

In short, it's when the conversation feels natural. I'm sure you've experienced a moment where you've had the best conversation of your life... It feels easy. It feels as though you can talk forever. It feels as though you've known this person for a long time. You can talk about anything and everything and still keep the conversation interesting. This is conversation flow.

To be honest, I still struggle with this, but I know it'll feel easier each and every time I strike up a conversation with someone. I know this takes time to master.

When you're in conversation flow, you both are on the same wavelength. You continue to exchange ideas and bounce back and forth with interesting stories and anecdotes. There are no awkward pauses, interruptions, or misunderstandings; you just seem to "get" each other.

Tips to Keep a Conversation Going

Keeping a conversation going with someone is not as hard as it mayse em. Here are a few suggestions that will help you:

- Askope n-ended questions.

- Go for the narrow-to-open method (this is when you start with a simple yes or no question to get the conversation flowing and then actively listen so you can buildupt oaskingope n-ended questions).

- Ask others to join you in the conversation. The more, the merrier. When there's a group of you having a conversation, it'll feel natural, fun, and less awkward.

- Don't offer long answers that have no substance. If you keep talking and talking, people might get bored and want to end the conversation. To keep it flowing, make your answers short and sweet.

- Be unique. Ask creative questions that feel different.

- Share empowering stories.

- Approach people who have things in common with you.
- Offer your thoughts and get feedback.
- Have positive conversations.
- Be intentional and purposeful.
- Avoid topics that are controversial, such as politics. People will have different views and opinions, so it can lead to an argument or misunderstanding.
- Offer your expertise.

Self-Affirmations for Conversation Flow

Here are a few affirmations that you can tell yourself in order to have more effective conversations:

- I listen respectfully to gain a complete appreciation of the situation at hand.
- My intuition guides me by letting me know when to talk and when to stop and listen.
- I actively listen and engage with the person I'm speaking with.
- Every day, I feel more comfortable having a conversation.
- I have mastered my communication skills and know how to speak to people.

- Anytime I'm having a conversation, I feel in flow and in my element.

- I trust myself and my ability to have an empowering conversation with others.

- Everyday ,my list ening skills are getting better.

- When the time calls for it, I am slow to speak and quick to listen.

- I always know the next thing to say to keep the conversation flowing naturally.

Step Four Action Steps

Inorde rt omast er your next conversation, here are a few action steps to practice:

1. **Practice active listening.** Make a couple of shifts in your daily life that will help you listen more intently during your conversations. Practice not grabbing your phone or watching TV when you're speaking with your kids or partner. Practice maintaining eye contact for the whole duration of the conversation. Use your body language to gesture. Every time you practice active listening, even in the quickest conversations, you'll get better and better.

2. **Practice asking the right questions.** If you're not used to asking open-ended questions because it makes you feel awkward to stay in the conversation, step outside your comfort zone and make a daily goal of asking questions that will continue the conversation.

Maybe set a goal of five open-ended questions and see how the conversation goes from there.

3. **Practice having a conversation with someone new every day.** This will get you outside your comfort zone and help you feel more confident when speaking with others. Pick up your kids from school and have a conversation with the parents. At the grocery store, have a conversation with the cashier or butcher as you pick up the items. Get to know them and practice active listening at the same time.

Chapter six is the last step in learning how to communicate effectively. It's going to show you how to become a master communicator, and is the last piece in the puzzle that is bound to set you up for success. We'll be talking about a few different things, such as how to deal with challenging people, disagreeing without offending the other person, and so many other great pieces. I'm looking forward to sharing what this last chapter hasinst orefory ou.

Chapter 6:

Step Five—A Master Communicator

When you talk, you're already repeating what you already know. If you listen, you may learn something new. –DalaiLama

To become a master communicator, there are a few facts you mustknow ,unde rstandande mbrace.

- **Every human communicates:** Effectively communicating is the main way we can live a powerful, purposeful life. If we don't know how to communicate with others, we'll have difficulty getting ahead in life and achieving success. We won't be able to travel, have a relationship, go to school, get married, buy a house, own a business, or make our dreams a reality—none of this would matter if we can't communicate.

- **Communication is a two-way street:** In order to effectively communicate, you need to have someone on the receiving end of your conversation; otherwise, what you're saying won't matter. The person you're speaking to can receive the information you're sending out, and they can do what they like with it and, if they wish, pass it on to others.

- **Communication success depends on understanding:** Having a conversation is one thing, but effectively communicating a message to get its point across is another. When you're communicating, both parties need to be on the same wavelength so you can understand each other and have a successful conversation.

- **There needs to be conversation flow and openness:** When having effective conversations, it is important to be open to how it will go. Allow flexibility and trust so the conversation continues to flow naturally. Sometimes in conversation, a ton of topics are discussed—that's okay. Allow it to happen the way it's supposedt o.

- **Communication can happen in a variety of ways:** Conversations are not only verbal. They can be non-verbal, through social media, email, text, phone call, online chat, or radio—communication can happen anywhere at any time.

Now that you know this, you can look in and around your life and notice how you communicate; you can notice that you send a lot of emails or text messages; you always use your body language to send a subliminal message; you're a master at maintaining eye contact and active listening. It's like your reticular activating system is in full effect, and you're paying attention to the way you and everyone around you communicate.

Maybe you also notice some of the flaws in your communication. You might be a bit fidgety due to feeling nervous. You might struggle with holding a conversation or ending it. Perhaps you struggle with maintaining eye contact because it makes you feel anxious when people stare at you. In any case, this chapter will help you become a master at communicating. It's the last step in the process. This is an important chapter—I'm glad you're here for it.

The Power of Language

Language, as defined by the Encyclopedia Britannica, is a method of communication in "the form of written, verbal, non-verbal and signals, that helps you express yourself" in a unique way (2019).

We need language, any type of language, to communicate with other human beings. It is a way for us to get our point across and to communicate a message of help, survival, and the like. Language helps us share our ideas, thoughts, feelings, and opinions in a way that is unique to us and our self-expression.

Imagine if you were in a conflict with your partner, and neither of you knew how to speak to the other… let's say you're English and your partner's Spanish, but neither of you knew each other's language. How would you be able to communicate? How would you be able to resolve the conflict? This seems virtually impossible, doesn't it?

So, you may wonder… Why is language important?

In the following sections, I'll be discussing the importance of language in various scenarios:

Language and Culture

If you desire to travel the world, learning languages is one of the best things you can do for your experiences. If you don't know how to speak the language of the country you are in, how would you be able to survive in the outside world? If you didn't learn about their culture, how would you know whether or not you are being respectful?

There are many ideas and opinions you can learn about a certain culture. For example, in some cultures, it is disrespectful for a man to glance at another man's wife. In another culture, it is customary to pray and take off your shoes before you step into a neighbor's house. And in another one, you must offer a kiss on each cheek when you meet someone as a sign of respect. Without understanding the culture and not knowing the language, how would you know this? By understanding the language and culture of a society, you can do your part to preserve the traditions and ensure they continue to last.

Language and Business

If you're a business owner, tell me something: Do you think you could get by and have a successful business if you didn't have a way to communicate? Do you think you'd be able to speak to potential clients about your products and services if you didn't know their language?

Being able to communicate is one of the most important aspects of a business. Regardless if you're servicing other businesses or fostering business-to-client relationships, it is important you know how to communicate effectively. As a leader, communicating with your team is also very important. You can share your ideas, thoughts, and opinions with them and get their feedback. They can share what's on their mind with you, and you can take their ideas into consideration.

On the other hand, if you are applying for your dream job, it is important you know how to effectively communicate your interest to your potential employer. In order to land the opportunity, you must know the best way to express your ideas, accomplishments, and accolades as they help "sell" you to your employer. Being able to sell yourself so you land your dream job is all part of successful communication between both parties.

Language and Personal Development

Understanding the importance of language has a listening component to it as well. Sure, you can probably talk your face off to another person, but being able to effectively listen and apply what you learned is half the job.

In chapter five, we spoke about the importance of active listening. When you desire to grow and enhance your self-esteem and confidence, listening to your mentor's teachings and applying them to your life is part of the battle. Actually, I would say it's most of it. If you had no idea what they were saying, how would you be able to take action on what you learned and also increase your knowledge and wisdom on the subject?

Language is an integral part of growing up and becoming a valued member of society. It is also an integral part of learning how to become an esteemed individual who exuberates confidence and unique self-expression.

Language and Personal Interaction

When communicating with others, do you think you'd be able to do it without saying a word? Sure, you can. You can use your eyes, hand gestures, write a letter, send a text message, or be part of an online chat, but guess what? All of this is still a form of communication called written and non-verbal. You're still usinglanguage but adiffe rent form of it.

When you interact with others one-on-one or in a group, you need to know the language to be able to communicate with them. If you're speaking on stage to an audience, knowing the language is crucial so you can get your message across effectively.

You can simply desire to share amazing news with your friend or partner, and you still need to be able to communicate with them. If you need to express emotions, such as sadness or frustration, you need to know how to express them so it doesn't come off as offensive or rude. Sharing the same language with the people you need to communicate to will greatly help you have a successful conversation.

Types of Language

There are two different forms of language in the way that we communicate: Oral/Written and Denotative/Connotative.

Oral/Written

Oral language is the verbal language we've been speaking about. It's the words that we speak directly with our mouths in order to spread a message or share some news. Written language is any phrases, signals, or other pieces of conversation that we want to share through paper format, either digitally or traditionally. Traditional written language can be in the form of letters or emails. Digital written language can be in the form of text messages, online chat, or direct messaging.

Denotative/Connotative

Understanding these meanings can help you use language with intention and purpose. Denotative is when you use a word in the literal sense. For example, if you were to describe where someonelive s,t he literal definition would be a *house*.

Someot her denotative examples would be:

- describing someone as pushy (they are literally pushing people)

- sayingsome oneisblue (they're literally the color blue)

- the person is pig-headed (they literally have a head of a pig)

Connotative is when a word or phrase offers a hidden meaning. It can have a positive or negative meaning, but the word or phrase is not taken in the literal sense. For example, referring to the word house, the connotative meaning would be a *home*. Home is where the heart is—it means security, family, dreams, love,t enderness, trust, communication, and care.

Referring to the denotative examples, this would be the connotative meaning:

- pushy means that they're bossy and maybe even aggressive—they don't take no for an answer

- sayingsome oneisblue me anst hat they're feeling sad

- when a person is called pig-headed, they are prideful andst ubborn

Language Elements

In order to improve your language skills, I feel it's best to discuss the different language elements that make up communication. By fully understanding and embracing them, you'll be able to become a master communicator in no time:

Clarity

Clarity is about having a clear understanding of what the speaker is trying to say so they can convey the message to the audience. If we're the speaker and we lack clarity in our message, the audience or the person we're having a conversation with can get confused, overwhelmed, and perhaps bored.

Less is more when it comes to clarity. When relaying a message, it is important to use simple, easy-to-understand language instead of technical jargon that only you can understand. For instance, if you're hosting an online program regarding wellness, people may not understand your teaching if you use terms such as chakras or divine feminine energy. However, they will understand what you're trying to say if you use terms like deep breathing, meditation, and self-care.

Word Economy

This is a term used in order to avoid the fluff and redundant language. If you try to get a point across by overusing words and over-explaining things, people may get bored, annoyed, and overwhelmed. It's kind of like they're thinking, "Get to the pointalre ady!"

In order to effectively communicate your message, it's always best to get straight to the point rather than beat around the bush. Word economy is about using your words wisely so that they are spoken with intention and purpose. It helps you avoid any fluff words that are unnecessary to what you're trying to say. If you make it a habit to let go of fluff in your conversation, you'll gain more clarity, and your audience will stay engaged.

Obscene Remarks

Swear words and curse words. Some people call it "colorful" language. There are many people who regularly use colorful language in their day-to-day life, but in all honesty, using these words is a bit unprofessional and, at times, disrespectful.

Imagine being a world-renowned speaker, and as you're speaking to thousands of people on stage, you drop a ton of F-bombs. Sure, it can enhance your character and personality, but would that be a good thing or a bad thing? For some people, you could potentially lose their respect as their favorite speaker because they could think that you don't really have class, and others won't mind your choice of language.

It is important you fully understand who your audience is before using these words as part of your vocabulary. If you're with your friends, these words may be appropriate because you're in a casual and fun environment. However, if you're having a business meeting with the CEO of your company, I would highly suggest choosing a different set of words in order to make your point.

Odd/Unfamiliar Language

You know how there are people sometimes who go on a rant about a particular subject, and your eyes glaze over because you have no idea what they're talking about? This is the type of language this is referring to.

When communicating, using unfamiliar or technical language can throw people off and may lose their attention. It's like going to your car mechanic, and he's explaining what needs to be done. Your eyes may glaze over because he's using technical terms you are not familiar with. It's always best to speak in simple, easy-to-understand language when having a conversation so you are both on the same page.

Influential Language

This could be used in a variety of ways: To manipulate people to do what you want them to do or to motivate, inspire and influence others. Many people try to use a manipulation tactic in order to make sure people know they're powerful—this is not a great communication tool. People may dislike hanging out with you, or they feel afraid of you… if they don't do what you ask,t hey're in trouble.

However, if you use influential language to inspire and empower your audience, you gain their respect and become an incredible leader to them.

Mixing It Up

When you use a variety of the elements we just spoke about to help get your point across. It helps make your conversations more smooth, and it helps you transition into different topics without awkward pauses.

Being able to do this well can be a challenge, but with practice, it can help you become a master communicator and gain a followingoflike -mindedpe ople wherever you go.

Disagreeing Without Disrespecting

In any conversation, we will have disagreements. That is a natural way of life, and in my opinion, it's what keeps conversations and relationships interesting. However, there is a difference between disagreeing and disrespecting someone while in the middle of a disagreement. There will be disagreement, but we must be cautious so we don't end up disrespecting them to make a point, as that can ruin the relationship.

Here are a few tips that I can suggest that will help you master disagreeing with someone while keeping disrespect out of it:

Be Open to Another Perspective

There are always two sides to every story. If you only focus on your side, that shows pride, which doesn't allow you to come to a mutual resolution. Being open to hearing the other person's point of view will allow respect from both parties and will show that you respect them enough to hear their side of the story.

Show Humility

When disagreeing, take your pride out of the conversation. The worst thing that you can do is be arrogant and pretend to dismiss what the other person is saying. If you come from a humble perspective and attitude, it shows that you are open to listening to the other side of the story. If you come from a prideful perspective, you are closed off and will only believe one side of the story—yours. This can show disrespect and that you don't care about what the other person is saying.

Keep an Open Mind

Remember active listening? This is crucial here. Keeping an open mind allows you to listen to the other person's explanation without judgment or criticism. Instead, it shows that you care about their opinion, and it is important for you to findamut ualre solution. When disagreeing, keeping an open mind is not always easy, as pride tends to get in the way. We are so certain that we are right in our perspective, and so is the other person, which is why there is a disagreement. If you both can learn to keep an open mind, mutual respect will always be at the forefront of the conversation.

Don't Go Into Attack Mode

Take your claws out of the situation and refrain from placing blame. When coming to a mutual resolution, it is important to hold ourselves accountable instead of pointing fingers at the other person. This is a sign of disrespect and immaturity, so the disagreement will continue to happen when these factors are involved. Find a mutual ground. Understand where the other person is coming from, and instead of being in defense mode, be open to listening and being present.

Breathe Before Speaking

This is part of emotional intelligence. Emotional intelligence is when you are able to control your emotions and not allow them to take control of your conversations. When we disagree, we are frustrated, upset, and even angry. When we are experiencing these emotions, we can say things that we don't mean and show disrespect. Before speaking, take a breath. Breathing helps you calm your emotions so you can speak with a clear head rather than speak based on your negative feelings. It allows you to take a quick pause and think about what you're going to say before you say it, which can help you avoid disrespecting the person and have a diplomatic conversation.

Dealing With Challenging People

It's ironic, but dealing with challenging people can be a huge challenge in itself. They know they're being difficult, but they can't help themselves. We will experience many of these types of people as we have conversations, so it is important to understand who they are and how to associate with them so you're not tearing out your hair during the conversation because they're driving you crazy.

There are four types of difficult people:

- **Negative Nancys:** The people who are always negative about everything. It's like they always have a gray cloud looming over them. It doesn't matter what you say—they always find a way to be negative about it.

- **Know It Alls:** The people who feel they are better than everyone else. Everything you say, they retort with, "I know that." They do whatever they can to make themselves look impressive, so you feel they are great people to hang out with.

- **Pushovers:** They have a bit of low self-esteem and will do anything that someone tells them to do. If you say, "move over," they'll move without hesitation. They don't feel their opinion matters in conversations, so they don't say anything and let everyone else do everything.

- **Bossy:** They tend to push people around as much as they can. They try to exert their power and manipulate others into doing what they want them to do. It is either their way or the highway.

So, now that you can identify them, how can you deal with them so you have a pleasant conversation? Here are a few ways that can help:

Stop Trying to Change Them

People with certain personalities are usually set in their ways. If you try to change them, they will only get worse and be more difficult to deal with. Instead, breathing can help when you're speaking with them. I have learned that in order for a person to change, they need to be able to recognize where they need to change and go on the journey themselves. If we try to change them, it only blocks their awareness.

Understand Where They're Coming From

If a person is exhibiting negative behavior, there is always a story behind it. Try taking the high road and understanding their story. If they're a pushover, it could be because no one allows them to talk or directly asks for their opinion. If they're bossy, it could be because they feel that's the only way to get their voice heard. Come from a humble perspective, and rather than retaliate and throw in the towel, try to understand their point of view, regardless of how challenging it is to speak with them.

Offer Them Respect

Even though they are difficult to deal with, it still doesn't mean you shouldn't give them respect. Treat them with kindness, compassion, and respect anyway. Try to refrain from judging them and making up a conclusion about who they are in your mind—you're only assuming they've always been like this. Still, offert hem respect because no matter what, they deserve it.

Use It as a Lesson

If you're feeling frustrated because you have to deal with a challenging person, look at yourself in the mirror. This could be a lesson you need to learn, and they are in your life to teach it to you. Maybe it's a lesson in patience. Or a lesson on how to overcome challenges. I believe there's always a hidden message in every conversation—in this case, the hidden message could be a lesson you need to learn in order to grow into a better version of yourself. So consider it as a blessing in disguise.

Self-Affirmations for Master Communication

To become a master communicator, here are some affirmations you can use to help you improve your communication skills:

- Iamapow erful and extraordinary speaker.

- My communication skills have helped shape many people's lives.

- Iamamast er at communicating my message clearly.

- I am confident to speak with anyone, no matter their stature.

- I am confident in speaking to difficult and challenging people.

- Ialw ays get my point across in a clear and concise way.

- My communication skills improve every area of my life.

- I have empowering relationships because of my extraordinary communication skills.

- Everywhere I go, I receive respect and give respect in return.

- Every conversation I have is a lesson and I embrace and acknowledge that lesson with every fiber of my being.

Step Five Action Steps

To become a master at communication, here are a few action stepsy ouc ant ake:

1. **Practice how you speak to others.** If you notice you curse a lot, try modifying your language. In every stage of life, it is important we find a way to grow. By modifying how we speak to others, we can grow into more esteemed individuals.

2. **Journal about the disagreement.** I find that it helps if you journal about the disagreement you are having. Take a moment to pause the conversation and give each other space to journal. Journaling can help calm your nerves and the frustration you feel, so when you reconvene, you are more clear and open to discussing the situation without disrespecting one another.

Conclusion

Learning how to talk to anyone without being afraid or thinking about fleeing is a life skill that will take you places—it can even help you achieve your dreams.

The lessons in this book will help set you up for success. I know they have helped me, so I can guarantee that if you take action on them and are consistent, you will experience significantimprove ments in your life.

As you can see, this is not just a book about overcoming feeling socially awkward; it is about learning how to become a master communicator so you can feel confident sharing a message and allowing your voice to be heard. I want you to know that your opinion matters, so by learning the key components I just offered you, you're able to take your communication skills to the next level—far beyond what you're used to.

Tore iterate, here are a few key things I shared:

- In chapter one, we spoke about the importance of communication when it comes to relationships. In order to make your relationships last, put communication at the forefront of your relationship. When you have communication, honesty and trust fall behind it.

- Mastering communication can open a wide array of doors in your life. When you know how to communicate effectively, extraordinary opportunities showupw hen you least expect them to.

- In chapter two, we spoke about the importance of self-esteem and how it plays into your confidence. When you exhibit high self-esteem, it shows in the way you communicate.

- Just the same, when you love yourself and focus on enhancing your body image, you allow yourself to shine fromt he inside out.

- It is important to advocate for yourself when working on your confidence. When you can be your own best friend rather than your inner bully, your self-confidence andc ommunication skills will increase.

- In chapter four, we spoke about focusing on our tone of voice and body language to send a clear message rather than one that exhibits confusion and the wrong impression.

- In chapter five, we discussed the importance of active listening and how being fully present in conversations will achieve empowering results.

- In chapter six, we are reminded to have an open mind when dealing with challenging people and to let go of assumptionssow e canhave ple asant conversations.

There were so many other great things that we went over, but these are just a few examples. I trust that each chapter has given you an extra bout of confidence, so when it's time for you to have another conversation, you will notice the changes andbe grat eful for them.

Thank you for joining me on this journey. If you know of anyone that is going through a similar experience and could use some help and inspiration to increase their confidence, I encourage you to share this book with them. I also encourage you to write a review on Amazon so I can know how this book hashe lpedimprove your life, and I can celebrate with you.

Iw ishy out he best of luck in your journey.

Here's to your confidence,

Joseph

References

Ackerman, C. (2017, December 18). *87 self-reflection questions for introspection*. Positive Psychology. https://positivepsychology.com/introspection-self-reflection/#questions-self-reflection

Anthony, S. (n.d). *How to keep a conversation flowing: The 7 best strategies*. Skills You Need. https://www.skillsyouneed.com/rhubarb/keep-conversation-flowing.html

Anthony. (2016, June 29). *How sleep impacts your confidence*. Inner West Orthodontics. https://www.innerwestorthodontics.com.au/blog/how-sleep-impacts-your-confidence

Apodaca, M. (2020, January 6). *How to deal with difficult people: 10 expert techniques*. LifeHack. https://www.lifehack.org/articles/communication/how-deal-with-difficult-people.html

Barot, H. (2021. June 7). *13 reasons why communication is important in life*. Frantically Speaking. https://franticallyspeaking.com/13-reasons-why-communication-is-important-in-life/

Basaran, Z. (2016, May). *The effect of recreational activities on the self-esteem and loneliness level of the prisoners as an alternative education*. Universal Journal of Educational Research. https://files.eric.ed.gov/fulltext/EJ1099797.pdf

Belyh, A. (2019, September 25). *10 reasons you should talk to strangers*. Cleverism. https://www.cleverism.com/10-reasons-you-should-talk-to-strangers/

Beohm, R. (2018, May 3). *From body image to body language*. Rachel Beohm. https://www.rachelbeohm.com/from-body-image-to-body-language/

BetterHelp Editorial Team. (2023, March 20). *What is imposter syndrome and how to overcome it*. BetterHelp. https://www.betterhelp.com/advice/careers/what-is-imposter-syndrome-and-how-to-overcome-it/?utm_source=AdWords&utm_medium=Search_PPC_c&utm_term=PerformanceMax&utm_content=&network=x&placement=&target=&matchtype=&utm_campaign=17990185911&ad_type=responsive_pmax&adposition=&kwd_id=&gclid=Cj0KCQjw8e-gBhD0ARIsAJiDsaVD4vXrHP0NvUChF2B7eHV_0mMzqoW2SeB94C_Jm9m17uDRvzmrEKYaAn-0EALw_wcB

Bhandarkar, S. (2015, November 10). *7 tips to master the art of disagreement without disrespect*. Essential Partners. https://whatisessential.org/7-tips-master-art-disagreement-without-disrespect

Bokhari, D. (2020, April 30). *50 self-affirmations to help you stay motivated every day*. U.S. Oral Surgery Management. https://www.usosm.com/employee/50-self-affirmations-to-help-you-stay-motivated-every-day/

Boogaard, K. (2016, September 9). *6 smart ways to disagree with someone respectfully*. Inc.com. https://www.inc.com/kat-boogaard/6-key-tips-to-respectfully-disagree-with-someone.html

Bradberry, T. (2017, May 4). *8 ways to read someone's body language*. Inc. https://www.inc.com/travis-bradberry/8-great-tricks-for-reading-peoples-body-language.html

Brazier, L. (2022, September 26). *How to get rid of negative thoughts and change your thinking pattern*. LifeHack. https://www.lifehack.org/articles/communication/10-ways-remove-negative-thoughts-from-your-mind.html

Bridges, F. (2017, July 21). *10 ways to build confidence*. Forbes. https://www.forbes.com/sites/francesbridges/2017/07/21/10-ways-to-build-confidence/?sh=58ebe5ef3c59

Clark, B. (2020, June 17). *Is F.E.A.R. holding you back?*. Copyblogger. https://copyblogger.com/f-e-a-r/#:~:text=F.E.A.R.%20is%20an%20acronym%20for,minds%20and%20pretend%20is%20real

Coleman, L., King, T. & Turner, W. (2021, July 26). *Six elements of language*. Southwest Tennessee Community College. https://socialsci.libretexts.org/Courses/Southwest_Tennessee_Community_College/Competent_Communication/12%3A_Language_--_Speaking_versus_Writing/12.03%3A_Six_Elements_of_Language

Conversations that connect. (n.d). The Professional Development Group. https://theprofessionaldevelopmentgroup.com/article/2011-11/conversations-connect

Coursera. (2023, February 21). *What is active listening and how can you improve this skill?*. Coursera Inc. https://www.coursera.org/articles/active-listening

Cuncic, A. (2020, March 21). *How self-esteem affects social anxiety disorder*. Verywell Mind.

https://www.verywellmind.com/self-esteem-and-social-anxiety-4158220

Cuncic, A. (2022a, November 9). *What is active listening?*. Verywell Mind. https://www.verywellmind.com/what-is-active-listening-3024343

Cuncic, A. (2022b, November 17). *How to overcome eye contact anxiety*. Verywell Mind. https://www.verywellmind.com/how-do-i-maintain-good-eye-contact-3024392

Cuncic, A. (2023, February 13). *Negative thoughts: How to stop them*. Verywell Mind. https://www.verywellmind.com/how-to-change-negative-thinking-3024843

Cynthia Ozick quote. (n.d). AZ Quotes. https://www.azquotes.com/quote/1265259

Definition of condescending. (n.d). Merriam-Webster. https://www.merriam-webster.com/dictionary/condescending#:~:text=%3A%20showing%20or%20characterized%20by%20a%20patronizing%20or%20superior%20attitude%20toward%20others

Definition of communication. (2023, March 10). Merriam-Webster. https://www.merriam-webster.com/dictionary/communication#:~:text=%3A%20a%20process%20by%20which%20information,of%20symbols%2C%20signs%2C%20or%20behavior

Denotation. (2017, September 27). Literary Terms. https://literaryterms.net/denotation/

Eatough, E. (2021, September 9). *Eye contact is important (crucial really) in communication*. BetterUp.

https://www.betterup.com/blog/why-is-eye-contact-important

11 remarkable workplace communication statistics to know. (n.d.). Apollo Technical Engineered Talent Solutions. https://www.apollotechnical.com/workplace-communication-statistics/#:~:text=Workplace%20communication%20statistics%20offer%20great,improve%20morale%20throughout%20the%20industry

Finding the right tone of voice in communication. (2020, September 7). Harappa Learning Private Limited. https://harappa.education/harappa-diaries/tone-of-voice-types-and-examples-in-communication/

5 important things to consider before talking. (2023, March 5). PrettyLifeStyle. https://prettylifestylez.com/5-important-things-to-consider-before-talking/

5 ways exercise boosts self-confidence. (2019, July 1). Jazzercise. https://www.jazzercise.com/Community/Blog/July-2019/5-Ways-Exercise-Boosts-Self-Confidence

Forbes Coaches Council. (2016, May 9). *13 ways to overcome negative thought patterns.* Forbes. https://www.forbes.com/sites/forbescoachescouncil/2016/05/09/13-coaches-explain-how-to-overcome-negative-thought-patterns/?sh=7d803fec35cb

Gipson, C. (2020, December 11). *Negative thoughts and their impact on your communication goals.* Better speech. https://www.betterspeech.com/post/negative-thoughts-and-their-impact-on-your-communication-goals

Grammarly. (2022, February 24). *The cost of bad communication is skyrocketing - What CMOs need to know.* Search Engine

Land. https://searchengineland.com/the-cost-of-bad-communication-is-skyrocketing-what-cmos-need-to-know-380456

Greer, J. (2022, March 31). *Ways to improve your body image*. Eugene Therapy. https://eugenetherapy.com/article/ways-to-improve-your-body-image/

Gustafson, K. (2019, July 7). *The relationship between confidence and creativity*. 3rdWave LLC. https://sparketh.com/the-relationship-between-confidence-and-creativity/

Hailey, L. (2022, November 9). *15 effective ways to connect with absolutely anyone, anytime*. Science of People. https://www.scienceofpeople.com/how-to-connect-with-others/

Hall, S. (2022, February 7). *The importance of communication*. The Chartered Institute of Payroll Professionals. https://www.cipp.org.uk/resources/news/the-importance-of-communication.html

Hanson, K. (2021, October 4). *357 communication affirmations to become a better speaker*. The Right Affirmations. https://therightaffirmations.com/communication-affirmations/

Harris, T. (2017, April 20). *4 types of questions to ask in a conversation to keep it going*. Radiant Hope LLC. https://www.theexceptionalskills.com/4-types-questions-ask-conversation-keep-going/

Hauck, C. (2019, November 13). *A 5-step process for befriending your inner critic to become a better leader*. SOCAP Global. https://socapglobal.com/2019/11/a-5-step-process-for-befriending-your-inner-critic-to-become-a-better-leader/

Hoque, E. (2015, August). *Components of language*. ResearchGate. https://www.researchgate.net/publication/327230822_Components_of_Language--_Dr_M_Enamul_Hoque

Houlis, E. (2023, February 10). *5 ways a lack of communication can impact your career*. FairyGodBoss. https://fairygodboss.com/articles/lack-of-communication

How does good nutrition relate to building self-esteem?. (n.d). Dehl Nutrition. https://dehlnutrition.com/how-does-good-nutrition-relate-to-building-self-esteem/

How dressing well can improve confidence. (2022, June 10). Monroe & Main. https://www.monroeandmain.com/blog/fashion-tips/dress-better-to-feel-better-how-dressing-well-can-improve-confidence/

How to keep a conversation going. (2020, June 17). The Cut. https://www.thecut.com/article/how-to-keep-a-conversation-going.html

Indeed Editorial Team. (2022, July 9). *How to keep the conversation going (with examples)*. Indeed. https://ca.indeed.com/career-advice/career-development/keep-the-conversation-going

Indeed Editorial Team. (2023, March 10). *Active listening skills: A key to effective communication in the workplace*. Indeed. https://ca.indeed.com/career-advice/career-development/active-listening-skills

Inner critic. (2015, August 10). GoodTherapy. https://www.goodtherapy.org/blog/psychpedia/inner-critic

Jim Rohn quote. (n.d). AZ Quotes. https://www.azquotes.com/quote/823805

Joanna. (2022, October 10). *Inspiring quotes about self-esteem.* Find a Way by JWP. https://findawaybyjwp.com/creative-life/reading-quotes/inspiring-quotes-about-self-esteem/

Keohane, J. (2021, August 4). *The surprising benefits of talking to strangers.* The Atlantic. https://www.theatlantic.com/family/archive/2021/08/why-we-should-talk-strangers-more/619642/

Landsman, I. (2021, August 24). *Understanding "tone" and its impact on conversations.* HelpSpot. https://www.helpspot.com/blog/tone-impact-on-conversations

Levin, C. (2017, February 6). *Dress to impress: Does suiting up bring more confidence?.* American Psychological Association. https://psychlearningcurve.org/dress-to-impress/

Lickerman, A. (2010, August 5). *The importance of tone.* Psychology Today. https://www.psychologytoday.com/intl/blog/happiness-in-world/201008/the-importance-tone

Marina. (2021, May 10). *Humor and confidence.* Kogan Coaching. https://kogancoaching.com/humour-and-confidence/

Marr, B. (2014, October 27). *How to start a conversation with absolutely anyone.* LinkedIn. https://www.linkedin.com/pulse/20141027073838-64875646-how-to-start-a-conversation-with-absolutely-anyone/

Mastroianni, A, Gilbert, D., Cooney, G. & Wilson, T. (2021, March 1). *Do conversations end when people want them to?.*

Proceedings of the National Academy of Sciences of the United States of America. https://www.pnas.org/doi/full/10.1073/pnas.2011809118

Meade, E. (2019, September 26). *What is positive self-talk?*. Positive Psychology. https://positivepsychology.com/positive-self-talk/

Mertz, J. (2012, September 24). *The importance of questions in conversations.* Thin difference. https://www.thindifference.com/2012/09/the-importance-of-questions-in-conversations/

Mind Tools Content Team. (n.d). *Making a great first impression.* MindTools. https://www.mindtools.com/a391uhu/making-a-great-first-impression

Mint Tools Content Team. (2022). *Active listening.* MindTools. https://www.mindtools.com/az4wxv7/active-listening

Moore, M. (2022, February 15). *How a lack of clear communication can affect your life, and ways to improve it.* PsychCentral. https://psychcentral.com/blog/is-lack-of-communication-a-red-flag

Morin, A. (2014, November 6). *Taming your inner critic: 7 steps to silencing the negativity.* Forbes. https://www.forbes.com/sites/amymorin/2014/11/06/taming-your-inner-critic-7-steps-to-silencing-the-negativity/?sh=5d8631b87feb

Morin, D. (2023, March 24). *How to keep a conversation going.* SocialSelf LLC. https://socialself.com/blog/the-5-best-ways-to-keep-a-conversation-going/

Motivation Statistics: Numbers in 2022. (2020, December 13). TeamStage. https://teamstage.io/motivation-statistics/

Murad, O. (2020, January 29). *Social anxiety in relation to self-esteem among university students in Jordan.* Canadian Center for Science and Education. https://files.eric.ed.gov/fulltext/EJ1241876.pdf

New International Version. (2011). Bible Gateway Online. https://www.biblegateway.com (Original work published1973)

Nichols, R. & Stevens, L. (2014, August). *Listening to people.* Harvard Business Review. https://hbr.org/1957/09/listening-to-people

9 Tony Robbins quotes about communication. (2022, October 27). QuotesGeeks. https://www.quotesgeeks.com/tony-robbins-quotes-about-communication

Norwood, E. (2017, October 5). *Surprising health benefits of smiling.* Henry Ford Health. https://www.henryford.com/blog/2017/10/health-benefits-smiling

Nuwer, R. (2021, March 1). *People literally don't know when to shut up - or keep talking.* Scientific American. https://www.scientificamerican.com/article/people-literally-dont-know-when-to-shut-up-or-keep-talking-science-confirms/#

O'Brian, A. (2022, February 8). *How to practice active listening: 16 examples and techniques.* Positive Psychology. https://positivepsychology.com/active-listening-techniques/#principles

Perera, K. (2020, July 13). *How does self-esteem affect communication skills?.* More Self-esteem. https://moreselfesteem.com/how-does-self-esteem-affect-communication-skills/

Persofsky, B. (2022, May 1). *Top 10 tips for communicating during a crisis.* Brown Brothers Harriman. https://www.bbh.com/us/en/insights/private-banking-insights/top-10-tips-for-communicating-during-a-crisis.html

Phipps, R. (2017. September 25). *Why is communication so difficult?.* Rebecca Phipps. https://rebeccaphippslpc.com/why-is-communication-so-difficult/

Prossack, A. (2021, November 5). *The power of asking the right questions.* Forbes. https://www.forbes.com/sites/ashiraprossack1/2021/11/05/the-power-of-asking-the-right-questions/?sh=20d67933217e

A quote by Dalai Lama XIV. (n.d.). Goodreads. https://www.goodreads.com/quotes/7062036-when-you-talk-you-are-only-repeating-what-you-already

A quote from The Dichotomy of Leadership. (n.d.). Goodreads. https://www.goodreads.com/quotes/9931489-there-is-no-growth-in-the-comfort-zone#:~:text=Quote%20by%20Jocko%20Willink%3A%20%E2%80%9CThere,growth%20in%20the%20comfort%20zone.%E2%80%9D

Rice, S. (2018, September 12). *Smiling is a social tool as much as a personal expression.* RICE Dentistry. https://www.irvinedentalcare.com/blog/your-smile-is-a-social-tool/

Robert. (2019, August 27). *Learning to "be yourself" with social anxiety.* National Social Anxiety Center.

https://nationalsocialanxietycenter.com/2019/08/27/learning-to-be-yourself-with-social-anxiety/

Roberts, E. (2012, June 6). *How to increase your self-esteem with self-care.* HealthyPlace. https://www.healthyplace.com/blogs/buildingselfesteem/2012/06/how-to-increase-your-self-esteem-with-self-care

Robins, R. & Crystal, D. (2019, January 10). *Language.* Britannica. https://www.britannica.com/topic/language

Sachchidanand, S. (2011, January 10). *Body image and social communication.* Nonverbal-World. http://www.nonverbal-world.com/2011/01/body-image-and-social-communication.html

Schaffner, A. (2020, October 15). *Living with the inner critic: 8 helpful worksheets.* Positive Psychology. https://positivepsychology.com/inner-critic-worksheets/

Schulz, J. (2012, December 31). *Eye contact: Don't make these mistakes.* Michigan State University. https://www.canr.msu.edu/news/eye_contact_dont_make_these_mistakes

Six elements of language. (n.d). https://saylordotorg.github.io/text_stand-up-speak-out-the-practice-and-ethics-of-public-speaking/s16-03-six-elements-of-language.html

6 interesting communication facts. (n.d). iEduNote. https://www.iedunote.com/communication-facts

Shashkevich, A. (2019. August 22). *The power of language: How words shape people, culture.* Stanford University.

https://news.stanford.edu/2019/08/22/the-power-of-language-how-words-shape-people-culture/

Stibich, M. (2023, February 17). *10 big benefits of smiling.* Verywell Mind. https://www.verywellmind.com/top-reasons-to-smile-every-day-2223755

Stosny, S. (2022, April 24). *How to discuss and disagree without arguing.* Psychology Today. https://www.psychologytoday.com/us/blog/anger-in-the-age-entitlement/202204/how-discuss-and-disagree-without-arguing

Suttie, J. (2018, March 29). *How to be yourself when you have social anxiety.* Berkeley University of California. https://greatergood.berkeley.edu/article/item/how_to_be_yourself_when_you_have_social_anxiety

10 steps to positive body image. (2018, February 22). National Eating Disorders Association. https://www.nationaleatingdisorders.org/learn/general-information/ten-steps

10 tips for active listening. (2018, May 14). British Heart Foundation. https://www.bhf.org.uk/informationsupport/heart-matters-magazine/wellbeing/how-to-talk-about-health-problems/active-listening

The secret of conversation flow. (n.d.). Dr. Dan LLC. https://www.improveyoursocialskills.com/conversation/conversation-flow

The state of business communication. (n.d.). Grammarly Business. https://www.grammarly.com/business/business-communication-report

12 ways to dress more confidently. (2022, April 20). Gigi Pip. https://www.gigipip.com/blogs/news/12-ways-to-dress-more-confidently

Van Edwards, V. (2014, March 28). *4 types of difficult people and how to deal with them.* Science of People. https://www.scienceofpeople.com/difficult-people/

Van Edwards, V. (2021a, January 19). *16 essential body language examples and their meanings.* Science of People. https://www.scienceofpeople.com/body-language-examples/

Van Edwards, V. (2021b, February 5). *5 powerful reasons why body language is important.* Science of People. https://www.scienceofpeople.com/body-language-important/

Vince Gill quote. (n.d). AZ Quotes. https://www.azquotes.com/quote/1374345

Waters, S. (2021, November 15). *How to carry a conversation - the art of making connections.* BetterUp. https://www.betterup.com/blog/how-to-carry-a-conversation

WebMD Editorial Contributors. (2021, October 27). *What is social anxiety disorder or social phobia?.* WebMD. https://www.webmd.com/anxiety-panic/guide/mental-health-social-anxiety-disorder

Why is language important? Your guide to the unspoken word. (2020, June 9). University of the People. https://www.uopeople.edu/blog/why-is-language-important/

Zetlin, M. (2015, May 27). *11 Foolproof ways to start a conversation with absolutely anyone.* Inc.com.

https://www.inc.com/minda-zetlin/10-foolproof-ways-to-start-a-conversation-with-absolutely-anyone.html

Made in United States
Orlando, FL
13 September 2023